NEW HAVEN IN WORLD WAR I

NEW HAVEN IN WORLD WAR I

Laura A. Macaluso

Published by The History Press
Charleston, SC
www.historypress.net

Front cover, lower right: Welcome Home Parade, May 24, 1919. *Courtesy of Robert S. Greenberg, Made in New Haven.*

First published 2017

Manufactured in the United States

ISBN 9781467136211

Library of Congress Control Number: 2016961481

Notice: The information in this book is true and complete to the best of our knowledge. It is offered without guarantee on the part of the author or The History Press. The author and The History Press disclaim all liability in connection with the use of this book.

In memory of my great-grandparents Albert and Mildred Paul,
members of the World War I generation.
"Millie" Paul (1896–1979) always remembered Decoration Day
and the doughboys who did not make it home to Connecticut.

Humayun Saqib Muazzam Khan
University of Virginia ROTC,
U.S. Army captain
(1976–2004)

Without memory there is no culture.
Without memory, there would be no civilization, no society, no future.

Elie Wiesel (1928–2016)

A poppy from Flanders field, collected and pressed by Elizabeth or Jennie Jerome. The poppy was adopted by the American Legion in 1920, inspired by a line from John McCrae's poem "In Flanders Fields," written after the second battle of Ypres in May 1915. *Courtesy of the Whitney Library, New Haven Museum.*

In Flanders field, the poppies blow,
between the crosses, row on row
That mark our place; and in the sky
The larks, still bravely singing, fly
Scarce heard amid the guns below.

We are the Dead. Short days ago
We lived, felt dawn, saw sunset glow,
Loved and were loved, and now we lie
In Flanders fields.

Take up our quarrel with the foe:
To you from failing hands we throw
The torch; be yours to hold it high.
If ye break faith with us who die
We shall not sleep, though poppies grow
In Flanders fields.

Above: World War I soldiers on the New Haven Green, circa 1917. These relaxed young men, not wearing their full accoutrements and not yet on the western front, but at home, are standing, just as the song says, next to "Church Street bright and gay." The New Haven Green was used during the war years for drilling, marching and exercising. *Courtesy of the West Haven Veterans Museum & Learning Center.*

Left: Sheet music, "When You're Down in Old New Haven Town, 1919." Music by R. Joseph Mazza (composer of "The Country Backs You, Mr. Wilson"), words by B.J. Orabona, published by the Liberty Music Publishing Company, New Haven, Connecticut. *Library of Congress.*

WHEN YOU'RE DOWN IN OLD NEW HAVEN TOWN

So you're leaving France today
For the good old U.S.A.
Let me shake you by the hand, "Soldier Pal"
Don't forget when you go home
Stop right off at my home town.
Give them all my best regards, "Soldier Pal"
Tell my best gal I'll be home
When I'm across the foam,
So good luck and good bye, "Soldier Pal."

You'll be sailing right away I have one more thing to say
Just remind me to the folks, "Soldier Pal."
Tell them I'll be home someday
And be glad enough to say that we won our victory, "Soldier Pal."
I can picture in my mind someone dear I left behind
Now she's waiting for me, "Soldier Pal."

Give my regards to my home town, give all my luck to the boys
Church Street bright and gay, Just like Old Broadway.
It cheered me up the day I went away.
Remind me to the old white way, where no one ever wears a frown;
Send a kiss to my mother and my love to another;
When you're down in Old New Haven Town.

CONTENTS

ACKNOWLEDGEMENTS

Thanks to Claire Ammon; Jason Bischoff-Wurstle, New Haven Museum; Margaret Bonaventure; Mary Christ, New Haven Museum; David Corrigan, Connecticut State Museum; Susan Clinard; Antony Cox, American Battle Monuments Commission, Brookwood Military Cemetery and Memorial; Sierra Dixon, Connecticut Historical Society; David Drury, author, *Hartford in World War I*; Michael Frost, Archives & Manuscripts, Sterling Library, Yale University; Kathleen Golden, Division of Military History and Diplomacy, National Museum of American History, Smithsonian Institution; Robert S. Greenberg, Made in New Haven; Harry Hansen Jr., department adjutant (Connecticut), American Legion; Pat Heslin, Connecticut Irish American Historical Society; Alan Jeffreys, Imperial War Museum; Ed Kacey, West Haven Veteran's Museum; Marie-Amelie Lebeau, World War I Centennial Commission; Stephen Leigh, American Battle Monuments Commission, Brookwood Military Cemetery and Memorial; Edward Mack, The History Press; Brett Morash, PhD, Bob Woodward Foundation; Libby O'Connell, PhD, World War I Centennial Commission; Katie Piasyck, New Haven Museum; Christine Pittsley, Connecticut State Library; Chad Rhoad, The History Press; Deborah Richards, Special Collections, Mount Holyoke College; William Sacco; Carlton A. Stidsen, New England Air Museum; Keith Stokes and Theresa Gutzmán Stokes, 1696 Heritage Group; and David Whaples, Yale University Art Gallery.

Huge gratitude goes to the wartime librarians of the New Haven Free Public Library who clipped and collected four folders of articles relating to

New Haven and the "European War," as it was called at the time. The term is still retained at the library as the headings on the file folders themselves, a small piece of history from a century ago. These yellowed pages have all but fallen to little pieces due to the acidity in early twentieth-century newsprint. This method of gathering information was eclipsed by mechanical, and now digital, technology, but this homespun way of preserving history remains useful and exemplifies the local. Presciently, a man from Boston named John Lowe wrote about this very act of clipping, collecting and keeping information six weeks into the war. In his May 21, 1917 letter to the editor of the *Republican*, Lowe wrote:

> *For the future, for the history of these days, librarians are planning a genuine service by way of gathering and preserving printed material which is so easily available now but will be in many ways impossible to secure later. For the future historian of the city or town a card catalog of all the men who enlist from the community giving complete and accurate data may be made as the days go by. Along this line also librarians should carefully preserve all printed matter showing any reference to the community in connection with the state or federal part taken in the war....* [I]*t may be a patriotic thing to be able to preserve in contemporary forms for the next generation the noble record of activity of the community.*

Although the names of the New Haven librarians who did this work during World War I are unknown, their effort survives here. Today, Alison Botelho watches over their work in the Local History Room of the New Haven Free Public Library—she is always helpful with my requests.

The name of another librarian is well known and well loved: that of Frances Skelton, who has been with the Whitney Library of the New Haven Museum for twenty-five years. I will sing Frances's praises until my dying day—that is how important good librarians are!—as her contributions are given freely and with good spirit. She herself loves "doing" history, and it shows. When I asked to see World War I materials, Frances told me she had found some scrapbooks so wonderful that she "opened the curtains...and soaked them in." As readers will see in chapter 5, libraries—and the people who staff them—bring so much to our lives, then and now. It is good to remember their service and their work.

PREFACE

Somehow I was in London on June 23, 2016—"Brexit" referendum day. I gave a short talk at the Britain and the World conference at King's College about monuments to Benedict Arnold and John André and took advantage of time there to look into World War I materials, exhibits and places in preparation for this book. Britain's vote to leave the European Union (Britain exit = Brexit) was based in some part on the anti-immigrant feelings that plague both sides of the Atlantic in the early twenty-first century. But few seemed to remember that the EU was born of the necessity to find ways to create and strengthen political, economic and cultural relationships after two world wars that destroyed land, animals, culture and people in numbers too massive and thus too abstract to grasp (seventeen million dead, twenty million wounded). Out of this cataclysm, the world map was redrawn and whole societies changed, resulting in tectonic shifts of global power that relate, today one hundred years later, to the current state of world affairs and even to the Brexit vote. As C.R.M.F. Cruttwell wrote in the opening paragraph of his authoritative *A History of the Great War, 1914–1918*, "The idea of European solidarity was no longer seen with even the deceptive clearness of a mirage." After seeing the 468 white marble grave markers at Brookwood American Cemetery and Memorial thirty miles outside London, it was clear that this mirage deeply involved Americans, too—then and now. World War I is one more layer in the history of the Atlantic—a history shaped by explorations, emigrations and immigrations, global trade in goods and people, invention and industry, capped off by

Brookwood American Cemetery and Memorial, four and a half acres managed by the American Battle Monuments Commission, Brookwood, Surrey, England, 1937. (*Foreground*): gravestone, "Here Rests An American Soldier, Known But to God." (*Background*): Memorial Chapel, designed by Egerton Swartwout in Portland stone. Located within the larger Brookwood Military Cemetery, there are 468 World War I American graves here, some 41 of which were never identified, including one Star of David marker representing Jewish American soldiers. In New Haven, Swartwout (1870–1943, Yale, 1891) later designed the Old Yale Art Gallery and the bridge connecting the Italian Renaissance building to Street Hall. *Photograph by the author.*

wars for independence and political and cultural supremacy. But the war had, according to American journalist Edmond Taylor, "in many ways…left…deeper scars both on the mind and on the map of Europe. The old world never recovered from the shock."

Much to my chagrin when starting this project, I had never spent much time learning the details of going to war. (I suspect that this is true for some Britons as well, although individual economic frustration was the foundation for the Brexit vote and not the collective memories of a century of war.) Students of visual and material culture, especially traditional art history students as I was, are not exposed to the breadth and depth of scholarship surrounding war history. Further, living in Virginia for the past four years reinforced the primacy of the American Revolution and the Civil War, both of which loom much larger in public imaginations here—certainly much larger than World War I, photographs of which seem antiquated, as though they are not from the twentieth century at all, but from a far-off place and time that you would never want to visit. These are grainy black-and-white images of young men in lopsided metal helmets standing in maze-like tunnels of wood and mud; horses and mules carrying supplies on their worn backs; dogs dragging carts of people or artillery over dirt roads; camels in the desert, one ridden by a blue-eyed Englishman wearing long robes; ghostly figures wearing bizarre masks with large round eye holes, insect-like, to keep out seeping gasses; men temporarily blinded by the gases (including Adolf Hitler) or suffering from shock with shaking limbs; nurses in starched white dresses and caps, with blood-red crosses and capes, standing perfectly still over rows of narrow hospital beds in long halls; massive zeppelins floating above the earth, the dreadful hum of the engines rooted in your brain from the movies; European peasants, still wearing wooden shoes and handmade shawls, their villages nothing but rubble; paper-thin airplanes with wobbly wheels and stretched canvas wings; huge crudely made ironclad tanks (Churchill called them "land battleships") lumbering over hills, slits for eyes, giant guns blowing holes in buildings that were already hundreds of years old; barbed wire, with *queue de cochon* (pig-tailed ends) everywhere (the Thirty-Eighth Division Welsh dragon monument at Mametz Wood holds such barbed wire in its claws, such was the endless entanglement on the western front); and men wearing finely painted metal parts meant to replicate missing eyes, noses and cheeks. Images of World War I are wretched to view, only to be eclipsed by the knowledge and images of the Holocaust less than twenty years later.

But here I realized the power inherent in studying this period, when change was coming so fast and furious it was almost freakish. (An unleashing of the machines of modernity was captured by artists of the time, especially in the work of the Futurists.) The unsettling feeling about these years comes from how close in chronological time it is, yet how far away it feels—at least to me. I was born exactly fifty-five years to the day—April 2, 1917—when President Woodrow Wilson asked Congress for a declaration of war, which

John Singer Sargent, *Gassed*, oil on canvas, 1919. Commissioned by the British War Memorials Committee to paint a large canvas depicting Anglo-American cooperation, American artist John Singer Sargent traveled to the western front in the summer of 1918. Sargent witnessed the aftermath of a gas attack, which he called "a harrowing sight, a field full of gassed and blindfolded men." The painting was intended for the Hall of Remembrance, which became the Imperial War Museum. The foreground shows groups of gassed men en route to a field hospital, while in the far background, a football match is played. *Courtesy of the Imperial War Museum.*

had already been raging for more than two years between Europeans. In other words, less than one lifetime separated me from those of the "Lost Generation," from my great-grandparents who, had I been a little older and interested, could have told me something about how the Great War felt and how that event reshaped their worldview. As an immigrant from Italy, I imagine my great-grandfather Albert would have had something to say. I am grateful to my aunt Margaret Bonaventure for sharing this memory with me, of his wife, Millie, remembering the doughboys every Decoration Day, which was an earlier form of today's Memorial Day federal holiday.

It is not possible to turn back the hands of time to have those discussions and to learn from primary sources—the people themselves who endured World War I both on the homefront, the western front and beyond (the last American World War I veteran, Frank Buckles, died in 2011)—so, we settle for second or third best, which are those objects that remain behind and those objects created afterward that are intended to help us remember. This book is not a straightforward historical overview of one city, New Haven, Connecticut, and its relationship to World War I. That kind of work was done well by David Drury in his book *Hartford in World War I* (The History Press, 2015), which offers a grounding in the role of the State of Connecticut and the war, in chronological fashion. Instead, this book has been guided by the objects found: photographs, mess kits, monuments, diaries, song sheets, trench art, paintings, the skeletal head of a mule, prayer books, ration books, posters, pins and one doughboy's well-worn boots—all relating to the story of New Haven and World War I. This book is composed of many stories told through the objects that hold memories of the era—a photograph of an aviator's body, lying under a carefully displayed American flag in the living room of his mother's home in the Westville section of the city; a monument to a first-generation Irish American doughboy who suffered greatly after returning from the western front, likely a victim of post-traumatic stress disorder (PTSD) and the effects of exposure to gas; a painting of a dog that may be the most famous "person" to come off the streets of New Haven and which participated in every major battle of the western front, earning more medals than his handmade chamois coat could display. These kinds of objects, spread far and wide, are small but precious reminders of an event that laid the foundation of the twentieth century, of our age of mechanized technology, globalism and world war and its twenty-first-century repercussions, such as the Brexit vote, which continue to shape contemporary life.

Because this approach is not exhaustive or exclusive, ideally more stories can be added, further broadening the many perspectives that make the whole. I'm looking forward to seeing more stories added via the *Remembering World War One: Sharing History/Preserving Memories* portal, a digital project managed by Christine Pittsley at the Connecticut State Library. Christine has been visiting locations around the state, meeting family members and friends of the World War I generation, digitizing their objects—those things saved and stored in shoeboxes, under beds and in attics—and uploading them for everyone to share and appreciate. She'll continue her work through this important anniversary year, and I encourage everyone to have a look and participate at http://ctinworldwar1.org. The Connecticut State Library, in fact, contains an unparalleled resource for studying World War I, but the bulk of the material is from and about Hartford. I'm hoping that with Christine's visits to New Haven County more family material will appear and become digitized. But there is another problem with this approach: because my methodology is object-based, those stories not documented and saved, either by private individuals or in public collections, are missing—and there are many of them. For example, Keith and Theresa Guzmán Stokes at 1696 Heritage Group have written about their ancestor First Lieutenant Charles Henry Barclay (see chapter 2), a member of the Ninety-Third Infantry (Colored) Division, but scant material culture of his life remains. Many African Americans from New Haven County served in the Great War, but who has saved memories of their stories? And what about the two women from New Haven, Irene M. Flynn and Helen Agnes Moakley, both nurses with the American Red Cross, who died in Europe? Beyond their names, who has saved their stories?

In terms of memorializing the centennial, the Allies of World War I—Britain and the Commonwealth, France, Russia, Italy and the United States, among others—are remembering their history during these centennial years (2014–18) in numerous ways. Americans are engaged in this process on the national stage under the aegis of the United States World War I Centennial Commission (WWICC), whose primary mission—Educate/Honor/Commemorate—is the design and installation of a memorial in Pershing Park, close to the National Mall, in Washington, D.C. After an open call for ideas, the design by architect-in-training Joe Weishaar and sculptor Sabin Howard was selected from 350 entries in the public competition. *The Weight of Sacrifice* will install three "processional walls" around an already existing bronze statue of John "Black Jack" Pershing, general of the American Expeditionary Force (AEF) during World War I. For those familiar with the National Mall and its long history of erecting monuments, beginning with the installation of the Washington Monument in 1848, know that traditional forms and materials are favored. This includes the use of marble, bronze, obelisks, allegories, equestrian statues, the Classical architectural style and realistic representations of human figures. The one stand-out—the abstract memorial that remains challenging, yet deeply personal (even for those who did not lose a family member or friend), more than thirty years after its installation—is, of course, Maya Lin's Vietnam Veterans Memorial (1982). *The Weight of Sacrifice*, with funds raised entirely from private sources, is slated for completion by November 11, 2018, marking the centennial of the armistice (or peace). The memorial brings together elements from both traditions of American monument-making: figures in relief of all sorts of people—and animals—will be incised into the stone

Robert White (sculptor) and Wallace K. Harrison (architect), *John J. Pershing, General of the Armies*, bronze and red granite. Pershing Square Park, Washington, D.C., 1981. Due to its location near—but also in the shadow of—the National Mall and the White House, this small park, bounded by Pennsylvania Avenue NW, has had its share of both over design and neglect. The current park features memorial walls with interpretive text about Pershing, with maps of the western front and American contributions to major offenses. A re-envisioning of the memorial will open in November 2018, the centennial of the armistice. *Photograph by the author.*

Paul Cummins (design) and Tom Piper (staging), *Blood Swept Lands and Seas of Red*, Tower of London, July–November 2014. 888,246 painted ceramic poppies were crafted by Cummins in his Derbyshire studio, where the artist found an anonymous poem that began "blood swept lands and seas of red/where angels dare to tread." About 17,500 volunteers placed the poppies, each flower raising £25, for a total of an estimated £15 million going to six veterans' charities. The poppies appeared to fall out of the "Weeping Window" on the Tower, one of London's oldest and most iconic buildings. *Courtesy of Deror_avi and Wikimedia Commons.*

walls, encouraging viewers to walk along, as in the Vietnam Veterans Memorial, witnessing the tremendous changes experienced from the beginning of the war to the end. Bringing down the bronze statue of Pershing to ground level, so that viewers might see (and, inevitably, touch) the monument, is a superb way of adapting older monuments to new viewers. New Haven's World War I monuments are discussed in the last two chapters of this book. Will the city and Yale University find ways to reinvigorate these bronze, marble and granite memory markers too?

The losses Americans suffered in World War I were horrible but pale in comparison to the staggering loss of life suffered by Allied countries such as Britain. Almost twenty thousand men—"the choicest and the best of our young manhood" according to Prime Minister David Lloyd George—died within the first four hours of the Battle of the Somme in July 1916. In the realm of remembering, the British rise to the occasion; their practices of memorializing are traditional (cenotaphs and poppy wreaths are common) but, in contemporary culture, also include temporary exhibits that capture mood, sentiment and gratitude in ways that are particularly evocative and emotional. Britain opened its centennial commemorations in 2014 with *Blood Swept Lands and Seas of Red*, an installation of 888,246 ceramic red poppies spilling out from the Tower of London. Each poppy represented one dead person from Britain and the Commonwealth, the title of the work coming from an anonymous poem from the war.

On July 1, 2016, hundreds of actors dressed in World War I "Tommy" (the British name for doughboys) uniforms swarmed public transportation hubs such as train stations, singing "We're Here Because We're Here" (#wearehere) to mark the centennial of the start of the Battle of the Somme, again an image coming from a poem of the Great War. (The phrase also echoes in American consciousness, as the first American Expeditionary Force to reach France came with the words "Lafayette, we are here!") Likewise, artist Rob Heard spent four years crafting *Shrouds of the Somme*—19,240 human figurines wrapped in linen, each one hand-stitched—to remember this day, the figures laid out in rows in Exeter near a World War I memorial. It remains to be seen if American memorializing will attain such visual impact and grace. American memorializing tends to be static and over-scaled, such as the installation of the World War II Memorial on the National Mall in 2005. Britain's choices of artistic and temporary memorials are effective in our age of digital technology.

INTRODUCTION TO WORLD WAR I

The world must be made safe for democracy. Its peace must be planted upon the tested foundations of political liberty. We have no selfish ends to serve. We desire no conquest, no dominion. We seek no indemnities for ourselves, no material compensation for the sacrifices we shall freely make. We are but one of the champions of the rights of mankind. We shall be satisfied when those rights have been made as secure as the faith and the freedom of nations can make them.

This is a war to end all wars.

—*Woodrow Wilson, president of the United States, 1917*

Called the European War, later the Great War and, after 1945, World War I, this was the first global conflict of the twentieth century. During this war, seventeen million lives were erased in the years between 1914 and 1918, and seeds of political and social discontent were sown that remain with us today. War is a part of human civilization, part and parcel of the conquest of people and ideas across land and sea since antiquity, but beginning with World War I, air would become a pivotal space for war-making as well. What makes World War I different is the "total war" concept—the number of countries involved, the enormous amounts of weapons produced, the new technologies developed (such as the tank and the use of the airplane) and the staggering death toll. While a certain romantic ethos accompanied many young soldiers to the western front in 1914, the poem "Dulce et

Decorum Est" by English poet Wilfred Owen demonstrates how quickly the experience shattered visions of patriotism and nationalism that fueled the war in the first place. Although it began in Europe, German and Austro-Hungarian aggression eventually turned outward across the Atlantic to the United States. The young country—only 138 years old in 1914—was already part of the conflict, using its strong manufacturing base to design, make and sell matériel (a word meaning all material things necessary for war) to both its allies and the belligerents, but America had not formally joined the war, keeping its isolationist stance for more than two years. During this time, the British Expeditionary Force (BEF), small in size compared to that of France, was decimated on the western front. Great Britain argued for the necessity of the American entry into war, but President Woodrow Wilson was hesitant, practicing his form of "non-neutral neutrality" until a number of factors pushed him and Congress to enter the "Dance of Hell," as one soldier wrote.

William Allen Rogers (1854–1931), "Watch Your Step," published in the *New York Herald*, August 9, 1914. Uncle Sam, with his eagle-headed walking stick by his side (notice the severe backward glance), sits petulantly on a rocky outcropping surrounded by bayonets and a thorny bush, trapped and unable to move. Rogers was critiquing Wilson's neutrality policy, which stymied Congress from addressing American involvement in the growing European calamity. *Library of Congress.*

Because the United States was making large sums of money from what historian Hunt Tooley calls the "sinews of war," unrestricted German submarine warfare in the Atlantic, which torpedoed military, commercial and personal ships indiscriminately—everyone is familiar with the story of the RMS *Lusitania*, which was torpedoed and sunk in only eighteen minutes on May 7, 1915, killing 1,198 people—began to wear down American resolve to stay out of the war. The discovery of the Zimmerman telegram in early 1917, published by the British government, finally convinced the United States it was not prudent to remain politically neutral. In the telegram, Germany offered Mexico a partnership if the country would

Paul Ducuing (French, 1867–1949), *WWI Trench Digger* (1920) and *American Soldier of World War I Carrying His Gun under His Arm* (1921), Sèvres, France, 1921. Parian ware (named for the Greek Island of Paros) is unglazed bisque porcelain—the white color imitates marble at a fraction of the cost. In the collection of four figures at the Yale University Art Gallery (only two are shown here), two are French and two are American—no other Allies are represented. *Courtesy of the Yale University Art Gallery, Gift of de Lancey Kountze, B.A. 1899, 1939.104 and 1939.106.*

invade Texas, thereby forcing the United States to fight a war in two directions. The potential alliance of Germany and Mexico incensed the American public, pushing Wilson, who had won his second term in office under the slogan "He kept us out of war," to ask Congress for a declaration of war on April 2, 1917.

Soldiers from New Haven, Connecticut, such as Philip English of Company F (later M), 102nd Regiment, 26th Division, fought mostly on the western front—that area of France and Belgium infamous for its static battle lines, or "fronts," that were literally dug into the earth in the form of trenches, bunkers, barbed wire, wooden planks and a "companionship of mud." English called the front "this narrow belt of world hatred stretched

Combined flag of the Allies, War Records Department Historical Data, RG 12. The Allies of World War I were a military alliance with political overtones originally led by the "Triple Entente" of Great Britain, France and Russia. They were joined by Italy (which changed sides after 1915), Greece, Romania, Montenegro, Belgium, Serbia and Japan. The United States, Canada, Brazil, Portugal, China, Australia, South Africa, New Zealand and Siam (Thailand) later entered the war on the side of the Allies. In sum, thirty countries from five continents were involved. *Courtesy of the Connecticut State Library.*

for 400 miles." But World War I also touched deeply the Middle East, North Africa and Russia and included Commonwealth countries (those attached to Great Britain) India, Canada, Australia and New Zealand. Japan was an ally as well. This was a total, global war the likes of which had never been seen before. America's soldiers, fresh from the farm, factory or office, were far behind Europeans in military size, organization and strategy. But they quickly overcame their deficiencies to contribute not only materiality to the cause but also manpower and strategy, which helped to overwhelm the stalemate of the western front, turning the tide of war to the Allies by mid-1918. Two Parian ware statues in the collection of the Yale University Art Gallery demonstrate the importance of the French army on the impressionable young Americans. In 1917, French infantry, called *poilus* (meaning "hairy ones"), had American regiments attached to them so that they might learn trench warfare on the front, while American aviators were often attached to French *escadrilles* (air squadrons) in order to replenish their numbers. Upon meeting the French, New Havener Gilbert Nelson Jerome wrote:

> *We have met all sorts of interesting characters. Especially the French soldiers lay themselves out to be hospitable. On the train we fraternized with some soldiers, drank red wine out of their canteens, shared our lunch and had a convivial time. I gave my harmonica to one of these chaps who took a fancy to it. In return he tried to give us his* Croix de Guerre, *which he had won for bravery. Of course we didn't take it.*

Here, a *poilu* is shown digging a trench, while the doughboy (an American infantry soldier who wore brown wrappings on his lower legs called "puttees") walks calmly, a German *pickelhaube* (spiked combat helmet made of boiled leather) in his left hand and his rifle under his right arm. On the eleventh hour of the eleventh day of the eleventh month—November 11, 1918—the Armistice of Compiègne, named for the forest on the western front, was signed, signaling the cessation of hostilities. Six months later (and five years after the assassination of Archduke Franz Ferdinand of Austria), the Paris Peace Conference produced the Treaty of Versailles, outlining the deep reparations—both psychological and monetary—Germany would be forced to pay for its leading role in the war.

The potential stories about World War I seem endless; for every American city (let alone every European city and beyond), there are histories and memories hidden in museums, archives and private collections in abundance. The centennial year of the American entry into World War I will excavate some of these histories and memories, monuments will get much-needed conservation treatments and maintenance and the long-neglected global event will enter our consciousness again, at least for a few moments. New Haven, Connecticut, a small city located on Long Island Sound, halfway between New York City and Boston, is one of those places with many stories to tell. The war changed the city; the walls between town and gown were dissolved, societal and cultural ties were strengthened and a solid sense of American identity, service and patriotism in the form of Uncle Sam took hold and remain with us, still. Some of the changes lasted longer than others. Winchester Repeating Arms Manufactory, for example, a powerhouse of munitions during World War I, shut down in the 1930s (only to be revived during World War II), while the walls between Yale University and the City of New Haven were literally and figuratively rebuilt higher in the 1930s, a legacy that the city deals with to this day. Young women got the chance to do things never before offered—a pharmacy course was available at New Haven High School for sixty dollars, as the city needed pharmacy assistants to replace the city's "draft men." Other women in New Haven, such as Katherine Mullen, a leader in the Girls' Patriotic League, used their organizational and community-building skills to fight for suffrage, finally granted in 1920. Some of the histories and memories of New Haven and World War I are brought forward here, utilizing public and private collections and public spaces around the city, from grave sites and public parks to monuments and memorials, all asking us to remember them. The story of a Gold Star mother from New Haven begins this journey.

1

A GOLD STAR PILGRIMAGE

The Jerome Family of New Haven

In September 1919, an older woman and her daughter, both in long black dresses with white lace collars and cuffs, stood together at a grave site in the Argonne, an area of rocky mountain and forest in northeastern France, near Belgium. Numerous crosses decorated the area. Together, mother and daughter had made a special kind of pilgrimage that is relatively unknown today but was undertaken by many women at the time. Elizabeth Maude Jerome and Jennie Gilbert Jerome had traveled from their home in the Westville section of New Haven to a village called Blâmont in order to see the places their son and brother, Lieutenant Gilbert Nelson Jerome, had lived and died as an aviator flying with the French escadrille Spad 90. During the 1920s, following World War I, the Gold Star Mothers Association worked with Congress to enact legislation enabling more than seventeen thousand American mothers to travel overseas to visit the grave sites of their sons. Congress was moved to offer such pilgrimages to Gold Star mothers due to the high number of soldiers buried in the European countries in which they died. In the early twentieth century, death during wartime was not as organized as it appears today. During the Great War, the bodies of thousands of soldiers were never identified—necessitating the widespread use of the identification or double "dog tag" system, and so, too, the creation of national cemeteries across the Atlantic in England, France and Belgium.

Gilbert's mother, Elizabeth Maude Jerome, and sister, Jennie Gilbert Jerome, wanted to visit all of the sites associated with his life and death, but they also wanted to bring his body home to New Haven. His body

Elizabeth Maude Jerome standing next to her son Gilbert Nelson Jerome's grave site in the Argonne, France, 1919. Elizabeth stands with the "White Wooden Cross." These temporary crosses, called the "highest decoration," were whitewashed and stenciled with names and dates and would eventually be replaced with marble in permanent military cemeteries both overseas and at home. Jerome's first burial site was behind enemy lines in the German military cemetery at Blâmont; he was moved here after the armistice. *Courtesy of the Mount Holyoke College Archives and Special Collections.*

> *In spite of the fact that we are far from the front, no one here seems to cherish any illusions as to the glory of war. There is a lot of joking about what we are going to do and what is going to happen to us, but the consensus of opinion is that there is no place like the old U.S.*
>
> *—Gilbert Nelson Jerome to his mother,*
> *Elizabeth Maude Jerome,*
> *November 15, 1917*

was buried and reburied again before coming to its third and final rest in Evergreen Cemetery in New Haven. The Jeromes undertook this trip long before legislation gave them any funding—the Seventy-First Congress authorized the bill in 1929, enacted in 1930, but mother and daughter went abroad in 1919, a pilgrimage more than a year in the making. From an upper-middle-class family that traced its roots to the founding of the New Haven Colony in the seventeenth century, Elizabeth Maude Jerome was able to finance the trip on her own. It is likely mother and daughter made plans for the pilgrimage from the moment they learned that Gilbert's plane had been shot down by German antiaircraft guns on July 11, 1918—exactly four months before the end of the war. For one month, Gilbert had been reported missing in action, but Elizabeth and Jennie learned of his death on August 15, reported to them by the American Red Cross.

The last time Elizabeth set eyes on her son, Gilbert, was two years earlier, in early September 1917. Gilbert was in Fort Wood, New York, for three weeks, procuring his equipment before setting sail for France on September 8. He came to visit New Haven in an airplane but drove his motorcycle from the airfield to his mother's house at 987 Forest Road (today Route 122), a large Colonial Revival with Palladian windows built in 1914 where the Jeromes kept their family heirlooms and dated Victorian furniture. Gilbert lived there during his two years working as New Haven's first Boy Scouts of America executive, a position he acquired in 1915. He had grown up with his only sister, Jennie, part of a close family, especially since Elizabeth Maude and Gilbert's father, Yuan Phou Lee, had a broken marriage. Lee was a Chinese student, later lecturer and scholar, at Yale University and appeared in New Haven as one of the first Chinese students brought to the Elm City for cultural exchange. Gilbert and Jennie saw nothing of him—they were raised by their mother and grandmother. But the house in New Haven and his mother standing in the garden were with Gilbert in the form of a small snapshot, which he carried with him in his

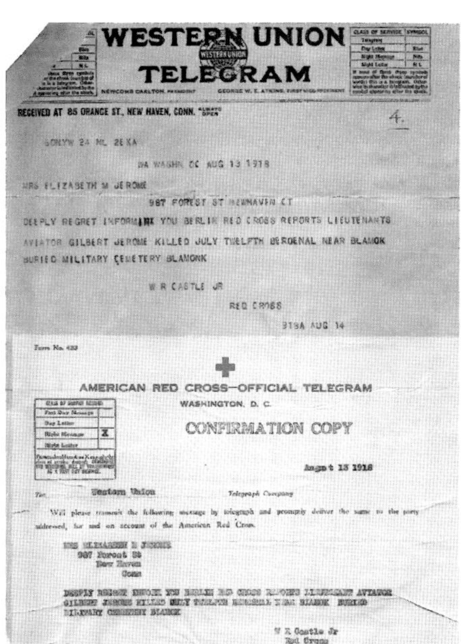

WESTERN UNION TELEGRAM

NEWCOMB CARLTON, PRESIDENT GEORGE W. E. ATKINS, FIRST VICE-PRESIDENT

RECEIVED AT 85 ORANGE ST., NEW HAVEN, CONN.

4.

5CNYW 24 NL 2E KA

9A WASHN DC AUG 13 1918

MRS ELIZABETH M JEROME

987 FOREST ST NEWHAVEN CT

DEEPLY REGRET INFORMING YOU BERLIN RED CROSS REPORTS LIEUTENANTS AVIATOR GILBERT JEROME KILLED JULY TWELFTH BEROENAL NEAR BLAMOK BURIED MILITARY CEMETERY BLAMONK

W R CASTLE JR

RED CROSS

919A AUG 14

Form No. 432

AMERICAN RED CROSS—OFFICIAL TELEGRAM

WASHINGTON, D. C.

CONFIRMATION COPY

Class of service desired	
Fast Day Message	
Day Letter	
Night Message	X
Night Letter	

August 13 1918

To Western Union Telegraph Company

Will please transmit the following message by telegraph and promptly deliver the same to the party addressed, for and on account of the American Red Cross.

[illegible]

987 Forest St

New Haven

Conn

[illegible]

W R Castle Jr

Red Cross

Western Union telegram and American Red Cross confirmation telegram to Elizabeth Maude Jerome, telling her of the death of her only son, Gilbert Nelson Jerome, in France, July 12, 1918. (The date is wrong.) The Berlin Red Cross staff alerted the American Red Cross staff of his death. Both telegrams arrived at the Western Union Office in New Haven on the same day, although the Red Cross confirmation telegram came in the evening. The Western Union Office was located on Orange Street. *Courtesy of the Whitney Library, New Haven Museum.*

Greenway, the Jerome family home, 987 Forest Road (Westville), New Haven. Many of the houses in this neighborhood were built after the death of Donald Grant Mitchell in 1908, who designed Edgewood Park in the 1880s. Mitchell lived on Forest Road himself, choosing the area for its great natural beauty. According to urban historian Elizabeth Mills Brown, the houses here were "comfortably scaled, pleasantly planted…a beautifully preserved specimen of upper-middle- class development in the serene days before the Depression.… [P]eople interested in the World War I period and 20s will enjoy exploring the area." *Photography by William Sacco.*

pocket, perhaps under the gold wings signaling his status as an aviator. About this house, called Greenway, Gilbert wrote to his mother and sister:

> *I picture the house and garden as they looked last September just before I sailed, everything balmy and blossoming. Then again I close my eyes and see the fire in the fireplace and think I hear the old grafonola* [phonograph record player made by Columbia] *again. You have no idea what home can mean until you have lived in camps and barracks for so long. Keep the home fires burning for me.*

Twenty-eight years old when he joined the U.S. Army Aviation Section, Signal Officers Reserve Corps, Gilbert's short life was filled with the kinds of education and experiences that prepared him well to become a "flying scout," an elite group of commissioned officers, many of whom were graduates of Ivy League colleges. Although Gilbert had attended Sheffield Scientific School, part of Yale College, and earned a bachelor's degree in electrical engineering, he was also a product of the New Haven

Christmas card drawn and painted by Gilbert Nelson Jerome, unknown date. Gilbert was the first Boy Scout in New Haven and was soon appointed Scoutmaster for the city. One Connecticut Scout leader wrote, "He knows more about Scout work than any man I ever knew and I have known a great many." Gilbert's personal mottoes were "social service" and "be prepared." The American Scout uniform resembled an aviator's uniform—although a patch on the left arm (a large fleur-de-lis) would denote his status as part of the new worldwide movement of self-improvement for boys. *Courtesy of the Whitney Library, New Haven Museum.*

Your picture is a great delight; also a little one of you standing in the garden at summer time. I carry this last one in my pocket-book and often dream of home…keep the home fires burning for me.

—Gilbert Nelson Jerome to his mother, Elizabeth Maude Jerome, March 8, 1918

public school system, having graduated from New Haven High School in 1907. After Yale, Gilbert, a devoted Christian who attended Plymouth Congregational Church on Chapel Street, went to study humanics (the study of emotional, intellectual and physical lives) at the International YMCA College in Springfield, Massachusetts, where he received a second bachelor's degree in 1914. At the same time, Gilbert threw himself into the Scouting movement in New Haven and was the city's first Boy Scout—eventually becoming its first administrator, after graduating from Springfield.

In addition to Gilbert's study of technology and psychology, the young man had, since childhood, practiced art in the form of drawing, painting watercolors and writing poetry. That Gilbert was encouraged to develop this aspect of his interest is not surprising—his grandmother, also named Elizabeth, was an accomplished portrait artist in Hartford in the 1860s and 1870s, having studied with Emanuel Leutze. (Leutze is most well known for his iconic 1851 painting *Washington Crossing the Delaware*, today at the Metropolitan Museum of Art in New York City.) Letters sent to his sister, Jennie, with whom he was especially close, are often accompanied by doodles and small illustrations, a practice he continued when he enlisted in 1917. A few watercolor illustrations also exist, including scenes from France—which was, in fact, his first time out of the country. Under his photograph in the 1914 *Massasoit* yearbook from Springfield, Gilbert was characterized as follows: "[G]iven a piece of crayon, a blackboard, and an audience, there is no story he cannot tell convincingly and illustrate perfectly. And, moreover he is a student and a philosopher." His mother described Gilbert as a beautiful child with whose hands "were long and delicately molded, showing his artistic temperament." Although Gilbert enjoyed drawing and painting small scenes from life, his real interest was in the modern machinery with which he became enamored—especially the airplane.

When Gilbert learned to fly in 1917, the biplane was a celebrated and romantic entry into World War I. Both the Allies and the Central powers strained to gain control of the air through the training of new pilots and, likewise, by shooting enemy aircraft down with antiaircraft guns. Gilbert had foreseen the use of airplanes in war; he wrote a paper while a student at New Haven High School called the "Battle of the Airships." But he also anticipated the development of airplanes for more than war use. In a letter to his mother from France, Gilbert wrote, "After the war, I predict a great boom in the use of airplanes for carrying mail, etc." After he enlisted, Gilbert headed to Ground School at MIT in Cambridge to begin eight weeks of training, after which he and two other men were sent to Tours, France, for three months of "practical aviation." Gilbert had been on an airplane only once before—as a tourist in Miami—but his fascination with planes comes across clearly in a poem he wrote in January 1918 that appeared in the Paris edition of the *New York Herald.* Gilbert's poem (in the vein of the "warrior poet") came in fifth out of five hundred entries and won the up-and-coming aviator a prize of one hundred francs. After more studies at Issoudun and the French School of Aerial Gunnery at Cazaux, Gilbert was commissioned a first lieutenant. The first thing he purchased was a tailor-made uniform on which to pin his wings. Not able to give specific geographic locales to his mother and sister when stationed in France, Gilbert signed his letters from "Somewhere up in the air."

The Airplane

What strange device is this;
This thing of metal, wood, and cloth,
So cunningly contrived, and gay with colors bright,
Standing along out on the grassy plain?
Inert and lifeless on its wheels and skid,
Flaunting its glitter to the sun and sky,
It seems some giant's toy rather than
The latest product of the mind of man.

And now one comes and grasps the twisted wood,
And with a sudden swing exerts his strength,
His puny human force, there in the face
Of that brute thing, that mass of steel and brass,
When, lo, a miracle is wrought! Pulsating life
Is born, and from the heart of it
Bursts forth a might roar, a storm of sound,
So that the framework shakes and trembles on the ground.

Then, bounding from their hands like some wild thing
Seeking escape from bonds intolerable,
It courses o'er the ground and leaps into the air,
Spurning the lowly earth. Up, up, into the blue
It beats its forward way, until the mighty roar
Fades with the height into a distant drone,
A ceaseless hum, as if some monstrous bee,
Warmed by the summer sun, was flying free.

Thus, godlike, alone, the human being,
Loose from the fetters that for ages long
Have bound his kind to earth, rushes through space
And with a touch controls the soaring planes;
Bends to his will the pent-up power that beats
With frenzied force against the steely walls,
Hurling each piston back until the screw
Cuts the clear air in wisps of vibrant blue.

Such is the miracle of flight; the latest proof
That smoldering deep within the soul of man,
Half-buried ofttimes by the clods which mark
Him still a beast, there lurks the sacred flame,
The will to shape this star dust at his feet
To serve his end, lifting himself thereby until,
Freed from his heritage of passion, fear, and strife,
He mounts to better things, to richer, fuller life.

American aviators attached to the French escadrilles (small squadrons) used biplanes called "Spads" from the name *Société Pour L'Aviation et ses Dérivés*, a company that produced a number of design variations beginning in 1915. These small, light planes were developed for reconnaissance, in essence, to provide aerial viewing across enemy lines. Described as a "new weapon… which brought back the personal exploit of the individual warrior," airplanes were the "very eyes of the Army" and could also be used to shoot down blimps. The peril of flying under enemy fire—in objects made of wood and canvas—was known at the time to be a high risk, but for many, such as Gilbert, the powerful draw of flying overwhelmed the gamble, so much so that many Americans joined the British and French armies before 1917 in order to fly

Lieutenant Gilbert Nelson Jerome with his Spad XIII biplane. Gilbert described this plane: "[Y]ou see, a scout plane is the name given to the small, fast, one-man fighting machines." Spads were used specifically for flying over enemy lines and observing troop movement. They were painted with the French fighting cock on the tail; their top speed was 126 miles per hour. Although Gilbert said, "I am one of the most conservative flyers in our bunch," he only flew for a few weeks before he was shot down on July 11, 1918, behind German lines. *Courtesy of the Mount Holyoke College Archives and Special Collections.*

To My Son

A noble knight who lived and died gallantly,
I offer these few lines, a loving tribute from one mother,
Who gave her only beloved son for liberty.
In whom, many hopes were set, and justly.
In whose comradeship, love, counsel, in whose strength of
clear vision, and in whose memory, I find courage to press on.
All hail to such gallant souls, who count not the cost!
There are thousands of fathers and mothers who have lost
their loved ones, the hope of future generations, in this great war.
I am one with them in mourning.

—Elizabeth Maude Jerome, 1920

against Germany before the United States joined the war. Gilbert called them a "most marvelous collection of men and machines." Some of the young aviators flew for only a few months before being killed—some, like Gilbert, only a few weeks. The disconnect between the adventure and romance of flying and the dangers of doing so in wartime are seen in one of Gilbert's letters. He wrote, "[I]t is very odd to watch balls of smoke [from antiaircraft guns] suddenly appear in space out of nothing, and realize that they are meant for you."

In June 1918, Gilbert—called "Jerry" by his flying friends—was first assigned to ferry planes around France; he then was attached to the Eighth French Army and began reconnaissance missions. Three weeks later, he was killed. And in a way that could only be possible in a war with cultural underpinnings in the nineteenth century, Gilbert was given full military honors in a funeral ceremony attended by both German soldiers in uniform and the French townspeople of Blâmont. One resident of the village, Madame Marie Renard, who was the first to find Gilbert in his wreckage and later watched over the memorial at the crash site, helped Elizabeth and Jennie find the sites associated with Gilbert's short time in France. Perhaps the Jerome family name, which is French Huguenot, endeared him to the village or the fact that all mothers share a common bond. What is certain is that Gilbert himself spoke French, winning a prize his freshman year at Yale as a member of the Cercle Français, and that he appreciated greatly the experience of visiting French cities, towns and the seacoast before he perished.

Although Gilbert never lost his enthusiasm for flying, he experienced his own fate by proxy when his bunkmate and close friend was killed when his

The funeral of Lieutenant Gilbert Jerome, Blâmont, France, July 14, 1918. Photographs of the outdoor funeral service were taken by Boche (German soldiers) and the French residents of Blâmont, both of whom attended the ceremony. Professor Otto Schneider, a German army chaplain, spoke, as did Mr. Barbier, the curé of the village church. Gilbert's body would rest here—behind enemy lines—until 1919, when it was moved to the Argonne Cemetery after the armistice. A monument was also erected by Blâmont in the field where Jerome's plane crashed, tended by Madame Marie Renard. *Courtesy of the Mount Holyoke College Archives and Special Collections.*

plane crashed—the same plane that Gilbert had flown earlier in the day. Ernest Leach, the son of a Cape Cod minister, was not the only one of Gilbert's coterie to be killed in his plane; Quentin Roosevelt, the youngest son of President Theodore Roosevelt, was killed in action on the same day as Gilbert's own funeral in Blâmont: July 14, 1918, Bastille Day. Ernest's death prompted Gilbert to write a poem in which the first line of every stanza is repeated. "It cannot be. I say it cannot be," were words his mother and sister must have repeated to themselves for a very long time.

To Ernest

It cannot be. I say it cannot be.
T's but a moment since he stood

Here in our little group
And smiled and spoke.
A moment's flight and then
He passes thru the gate
That bars our view
Leaving us desolate.

It cannot be. I say it cannot be.
That he who moved among us
Winning all by deeds and words
Of quiet friendliness,
Has lived his few short years
Only to slip away
Into vanished past,
A sad sweet memory.

It cannot be. I say it cannot be.
Such friends never die.
He lives beyond the gate.
And when our turn shall come
To step across the threshold
Into a world more fair,
He will be first of those
Who meet us and greet us there.

When Elizabeth and Jennie made their pilgrimage in France, they visited Gilbert's crash site and grave site, various monuments, chapels and aviation fields—going so far as to retrace Gilbert's footsteps, following his educational route from Tours to Cazaux. Along the way, Elizabeth put souvenirs into her traveling trunk, including one of the wooden crosses from Blâmont, of which Jennie wrote, "three rude crosses witness bear, Is where my brother lies, here on this hill, with this wide view of hamlet, field and wood" (see page 156). In August 1921, the Jerome women arranged for Gilbert's body to be brought back to Forest Street in New Haven, where, coffin-bound, his body lay under a carefully draped American flag in the living room, surrounded by the furniture that he would have found familiar. On Tuesday, September 20, at three o'clock, a service was held at Greenway, and afterward his casket was brought by caisson and four black horses to Evergreen Cemetery, not far from the Edgewood neighborhood. Evergreen was the "new" cemetery on the western edge of town, as compared to the "old" Grove Street Cemetery in downtown New Haven. The Jerome family established a plot there when the cemetery opened in 1848. A spot was chosen by his mother directly next to her uncle Amos, who died at Fort McHenry during the Civil War. Gilbert had actually been named for Amos—the name in the family record held by Mount Holyoke College is "Amos Gilbert Nelson Jerome," though he did not use Amos. Both Amos's and Gilbert's gravestones were granite crosses—replicating the Latin cross markers in wide use in American military cemeteries. The inscription at the base of Gilbert's stone reads, "DEATH IS SWALLOWED UP IN VICTORY," from 1 Corinthians 15:54.

The family went on to remember Gilbert in both public and private ways, including creating scrapbooks of their pilgrimage, writing a book about his life and commissioning a sexpartite Tiffany & Company stained-glass window titled *Going West* for Plymouth Congregational Church, which the family claimed was the first "Boy Scout" window in the United States. Elizabeth called her son "my St. Jerome," and the central panel of the window featured an angel with the words "Death Is Swallowed Up in Victory" repeated from

Elizabeth Maude Jerome standing with her son's casket in the living room of their home at 987 Forest Road, New Haven, Connecticut, September 1921. Heavily carved Victorian furniture and portraits of family members reflect the family's roots, dating to the founding of New Haven. Gilbert's casket, provided by the U.S. government, rests in front of the fireplace. Jerome labeled one of the many photographs she kept of his wake "The Sacrifice." Boy Scouts and members of the American Legion came to the house for the ceremony that would take his casket by horse and caisson to Evergreen Cemetery. *Courtesy of the Mount Holyoke College Archives and Special Collections.*

Jerome family plot, Evergreen Cemetery, New Haven, Connecticut. Evergreen Cemetery, which looks across Ella Grasso Boulevard to West River Memorial Park, was created in 1848 as a new burial ground for the city. Evergreen became the site for the city's Fireman's Memorial and for extravagant memorials paid for with industrial money. Elizabeth and Jennie have the same gravestone design, although they died forty years apart. Gilbert Nelson Jerome and his great-uncle Amos Gilbert, who died during the Civil War, have stone crosses, similar to the Latin crosses in official military cemeteries. *Photograph by William Sacco.*

the gravestone. The Boy Scouts of America established the Gilbert N. Jerome Lecture Course for Scout Leaders and even today keep a campsite named for him at Camp Sequassen, in New Hartford, Connecticut. Elizabeth Maude Jerome died in January 1939 and, as with the attention paid to documenting her son's life and death, planned her own funeral, writing a "confession of faith" to be read aloud during the service, choosing the hymns and selecting the pallbearers. A Gold Star made of orange marigolds rested on her casket, and candles were lit under her son's stained-glass window. During the war, Jennie Gilbert Jerome, a graduate of Mount Holyoke College, worked to collect books to send to troops overseas. She became a long-serving New Haven librarian, first at the Dixwell branch and later downtown at the Ives Memorial main library. She died in 1979 and is buried near her mother and brother in Evergreen Cemetery, the last of her family line.

2

SUMMER 1917, CANTONMENT AND CAMP

New Haven's Enlisted and Drafted Men

Well before the spring of 1917, when the U.S. Congress declared war on the Central powers, the lack of strength in numbers of the American Army was apparent. While European armies had millions of soldiers on both sides, the United States had fewer than 130,000—numbers appropriate to "peace strength." At the time, there were 1,555 Connecticut men serving in the Second Regiment of the National Guard; they would be automatically drafted into the Regular Army to prepare for "war strength." When the declaration of war was announced, it was determined that more men were needed to enlist in order to fill quotas established by the federal government for each state and each National Guard unit. But before the draft, or conscription, was enacted on May 18, 1917, the Honorable George B. Chandler from the State Council of Defense in Hartford began a statewide public speaking tour to encourage men in Connecticut to voluntarily enlist. As early as 1916, the adjutant general of the Second Regiment said, "The main thing now is to get men. We want to get them now." With the mechanism of the Selective Service, by end of 1918, 2 million Americans had been sent to the western front, with another 2 million in training. Some 63,000 were from Connecticut. The scale of the effort—and the success of the American addition to the Allies—propelled the United States forward into a position of global political and military power.

The 2nd Regiment of the Connecticut National Guard, based in New Haven, had already seen action: in 1916 Pancho Villa and his Villistas stormed the Mexican-American border town of Columbus in New Mexico,

I Want You for U.S. Army, James Montgomery Flagg (1877–1960), circa 1917. Posters of Uncle Sam had a blank space under "Nearest Recruiting Station" where recruiters would fill in the local address. New Haven's primary recruiting station was 956 Chapel Street. The most iconic—and parodied—American image to come out of World War I, Flagg was inspired by the success of Britain's 1914 image of Lord Kitchener, pointing his finger at viewers, demanding they show their patriotism by enlisting. "Uncle Sam" became the personification of the federal government in 1813, popularized during the Civil War by Thomas Nast. *Library of Congress.*

and the 2nd Regiment was sent to Nogales, Arizona. After the incursion—led by Brigadier General John Pershing, later the commander of the American Expeditionary Force in Europe—the soldiers returned to New Haven in early 1917, just in time for the declaration of war with Germany. At first, the 2nd Regiment spent its time patrolling the New York, New Haven and Hartford railroad tracks looking for signs of sabotage—the Black Tom explosion in New Jersey in 1916 proved this was a real threat—but they were soon reformed with the 1st Regiment of the Connecticut National Guard to become the 102nd Regiment of the newly formed 26th, or "Yankee Division," based in Boston. Although the Mexican incursion was not a success—Pancho Villa eluded Pershing—the practices of camp life, long marches and weapons handling were the basis of training in the new cantonments and camps, preparing American soldiers for the war in Europe.

The choice—if there was one—to go to war did not come easy for many Americans, exemplified by Woodrow Wilson himself, a former university president and governor dedicated to neutrality. As in many towns and cities, there were residents on both sides of the argument: those making a stand for peace and those who believed in the necessity of war. The national argument played out in the Elm City in the form of a preparedness parade on May 23, 1916, that was publicly denounced by Professor William Howard Taft at Yale University, who was also the president of the Society to Enforce Peace. His son Charles left Yale his junior year to fight in the Great War. Marcus H. Holcomb, the governor of Connecticut, felt differently. In his "Preparedness Message," Holcomb said, "Marching in company with the heroic past, let us, in this untoward hour of world agony, face unflinchingly the menacing tide of events." In February 1917, Holcomb asked the General Assembly for the authority to make a military census of eligible Connecticut men and prepare an inventory of physical resources.

Although the doughboy, or infantryman, comes most easily to mind when thinking about soldiers and World War I, there were many ways in which men and women served during wartime, both on the homefront, the western front and beyond. In New Haven, for example,

Who's for the trench—
Are you, my laddie?
Who'll follow the French—
Will you, my laddie?
Who's fretting to begin,
Who's going to win?
And who wants to save his skin—
Do you, my laddie?

—*From* The Call,
by Jessie Pope, 1915

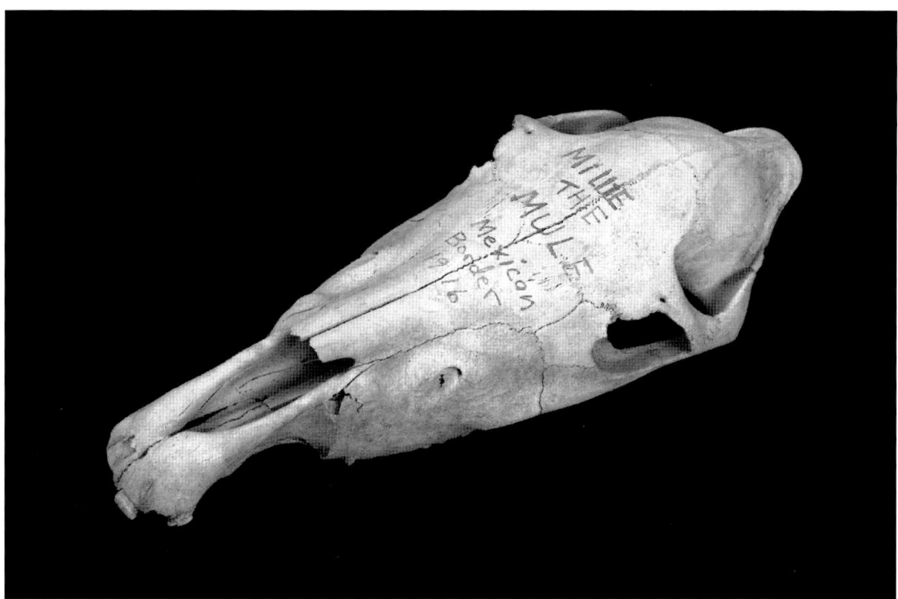

Above: "Mille the Mule," skeletal head of a mule, brought back to New Haven from the Mexican-American incursion, also called the Punitive Expedition, in 1916. While some National Guardsmen brought back sombreros (an example of which exists in the National World War I Museum in Kansas City), the skull—with a dried piece of grass still stuck in its mouth—was more attractive to the 2nd Regiment, an organized militia in existence since the eighteenth century. The 2nd was combined with the 1st Regiment to become the 102nd Regiment on August 21, 1917. *Courtesy of the West Haven Veterans Museum & Learning Center.*

Right: *Preparedness*, Paul Wayland Bartlett, bronze, 1916. Bartlett was born in New Haven in 1865, but by age sixteen, he was studying art and working in Paris. According to the Met, Bartlett began work on this statue the day after the sinking of the *Lusitania*. An erect eagle stands on a shield with American stars, with the word "Preparedness" under its talons. Bartlett also created the Lafayette Monument, given to the town of Metz, France, in 1920 by the Knights of Columbus (see page 114). *Courtesy of the Metropolitan Museum of Art.*

Governor Marcus H. Holcomb at a navy recruiting event in Connecticut, 1917. Holcomb (1844–1932) was a teacher, lawyer and later a corporate leader thoroughly dedicated to preparing the state of Connecticut for war, both in terms of manpower and the production of material goods. Under his administration, a Food Supply Council and the State Council of Defense were formed. After the war, Holcomb instituted a large number of pro-labor practices but denied women the right to vote—he left office five months after the U.S. Congress ratified the Nineteenth Amendment on August 18, 1920. *Courtesy of the Connecticut State Library.*

Colonel Richard North became the leader of the Home Guard Reserve, a contingency of men working in businesses, factories, stores and offices serving as a first line of defense before the regular army was ready to take over duties should the enemy strike on the homefront. The possibility of this was highlighted by the Honorable George P. Chandler of the State Council of Defense, who spoke at the rally on the Green, saying, "I come before you with all the seriousness and gravity that I can command, the grave situation that we face....Germany will come over here and invade the United States unless we hurry up and help France and England." The Home Guard Reserve was divided into three classes (first, second and third), with the first class dedicated to protecting businesses and properties from "enemies, vandals, and mischievously inclined persons," while the second class reserves were given the duty of temporarily repairing damaged infrastructure, including bridges, public utilities and transportation lines

Enlist now.
Your president calls you.
The army wants you.
The country needs you.
Come on you loyal Americans and lets free the world that our children may live lives in peace.

—Adjutant General McCain in a telegram from Washington, D.C., to the New Haven Recruiting Station, 956 Chapel Street, 1917

until permanent repairs could be made. The third class was reserved for men who, due to physical or other limitations, could not serve in any military capacity. Their duty was to "promote the spirit of patriotism and devotion to this country and state among their associates, and by their coolness in times of emergency, show their confidence in and reliance on the organizations which have been perfected to do military and guard duty." These men were likely candidates for the "DYB" or "Do Your Bit" clubs started around the country, working at recruiting stations to encourage local men in their churches, neighborhoods, factories and stores to enlist. According to one newspaper, it was "expected that every city and every town in the state will form at least one club, if not more." The purpose of a DYB club was to gather small groups of men, five to fifteen, to enlist together in a "spirit of fellowship" that would translate through to the front.

Before the United States formally entered the war, British and Commonwealth military units were another way for men and women from New Haven and/or Yale University to serve the Allied cause. (The French army prohibited foreigners from serving, excepting the Foreign Legion.) Americans fought in World War I from 1914 on—as infantry, in cavalry units and machine gun battalions, as seamen and as ambulance drivers with the Red Cross and American Ambulance Service. On the New Haven Memorial Roll of Honor (chapter 10), you can spot some of their names and the foreign units with which they served, including New Havener Eugene Donahue, who served and died with the Second Company, Canadian Expeditionary Force (CEF). To encourage American enlistment, foreign units would tour the United States. (Americans joining the British army became a criminal offense during World War II.) The Fifth Royal Highlanders toured New England in October 1917 to look for new recruits—the "Black Watch Tour" gained one thousand men according to one newspaper, including Jonathan Boswell and Donald Bothwell, both New Haveners, who served and died with the Black Watch division of the British army. A flying squad also visited New Haven that same month, and at least two recruits from the Elm City,

Company F, Second Regiment, Connecticut National Guard, was on guard duty at Winchester Repeating Arms Company between April and June 1917 before shipping out to the front. Fifteen men were stationed around the plant, with each standing guard for four hours and then resting for four hours. The guard slept in a wooden shed on site. Philip English described this duty as "deadly dull…nothing occurred to break the monotony of police duty." The Home Guard took over these duties once the Regular Army left New Haven for France. *Courtesy of the Whitney Library, New Haven Museum.*

J.D. Grant of 29 County Street and W.J. Houghton of 55 James Street, were both examined and accepted into "Kitchener's Navy," the colloquial name given to the British Royal Navy in memory of H.H. Kitchener, the secretary of state for war who oversaw the largest volunteer army the world had ever seen before drowning in 1916 when his ship struck a German mine. Americans were exposed to, and aware of, the death and destruction of the European War from newsreels, newsprint and propaganda—but, propaganda went in both directions: American artist James Montgomery Flagg was clearly inspired by the *Lord Kitchener Wants You* recruitment poster.

Another way New Haveners entered war service before the draft was to become part of the "Railroad Regiments," which were small regiments of skilled workers already working for railroad companies. One of these regiments was assigned to New England, from which ten companies were formed—one of which was based in New Haven. All prepared to go overseas to France in order to construct railroads and run trains for the Allies and the

Lord Kitchener Wants You, Alfred Leete, 1914. The image of Lord Kitchener, secretary of state for war who oversaw both a volunteer army and Britain's first draft in 1916, is said to be effective due to the foreshortening of the pointed finger and arm, which, along with his eyes, follow the viewer from any position. The image directly inspired the American version of Uncle Sam and later images, such as Smokey the Bear, who again points at the viewer, reinforcing "YOU" in the message. *Courtesy of the Imperial War Museum.*

upcoming influx of American soldiers. Newspapers stated that 163 men were needed for the following positions: stenographers, storekeepers, cooks, brakemen, engineers, firemen, yard foremen, electricians, linemen, gasoline engineers, draftsmen, surveyors, car inspectors, pile drivers, pipefitters, boiler inspectors, boiler makers, water supply men and blacksmiths. Of the 163 spots, all but 43 were filled quickly, with the blacksmiths being in highest demand. Men who wanted to join the U.S. military in this fashion were examined by Major William P. Wooten in New Haven and then sworn in.

If you were African American, your path to enlistment was different from whites. Charles Henry Barclay, for example, a forty-five-year-old man living on Ashmun Street in New Haven who made his living as an ornamental sign painter, entered World War I via a segregated National Guard unit. In World War I, the U.S. Army was not integrated, thus African American men who wanted to serve, such as Barclay, entered service in one of two segregated units, which, on the western front, were attached directly to the French army, carried French weapons and wore the Adrian helmet (see page 25) and an American uniform. The French army was integrated but, more importantly, was in need of able-bodied soldiers to shore up its depleting ranks after three-plus years of war. Barclay was a member of the 1st Separate Company of the 2nd Regiment, Connecticut National Guard, which became part of the 372nd Regiment of the 93rd Infantry (Colored) Division. It began its "great journey to the unknown somewhere" with many other regiments, leaving New Haven on July 28, 1917, for Camp Niantic. These soldiers served under the French 157th, or "Red Hand Division." First Lieutenant

Barclay served eleven months on the western front, suffered and recovered from a gas attack and returned home to New Haven. In contrast, most African American soldiers—more than 200,000 went to Europe—were stevedores (loading/unloading ship cargo) or laborers assigned to "service units," undertaking manual labor such as ditch digging, burying bodies and transporting supplies. These two African American units, though, proved their capabilities in wartime by earning numerous French combat medals, including the first two *Croix de Guerre* earned by Americans. As Theresa Guzmán Stokes wrote, "[I]t would be the African American citizen soldiers like Charles Henry Barclay, who would be willing to fight and possibly die for a country at a time when there were no guarantees for full citizenship, which would best exemplify American equality and freedom."

New Haveners were encouraged to enlist before the draft made the decision for them. The New Haven Green and other public parks and buildings around the city became sites for "big patriotic meetings" that were intended to stir up new enlistees and rouse the community at large. Across the state, seventy-one new recruits per day were needed. At one event in Wooster Square in June 1917, the Reverend Harris Elwood Starr, chaplain of the Home Guard and pastor of Pilgrim Church, and Sergeant Charles

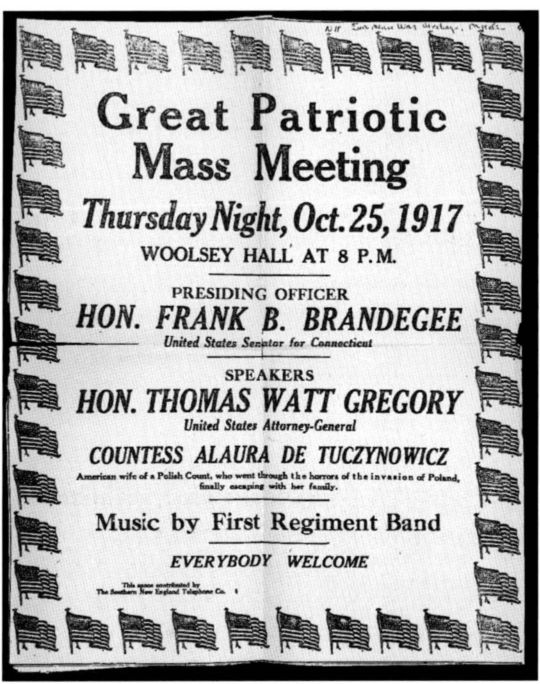

"Great Patriotic Mass Meeting" newspaper advertisement, October 25, 1917. This meeting was held at Woolsey Hall, a Yale University concert hall. Although part of the university, Woolsey Hall, constructed by Carrère & Hastings in 1901 for the university's bicentennial, played an important role in twentieth-century New Haven as a public venue for music, meetings, plays, religious services and memorial programs. Walking through the rotunda of Woolsey Hall leads to the university's war memorials. *Courtesy of the Local History Room, New Haven Free Public Library.*

M. Bakewell of the Yale Faculty Battery told a crowd of two hundred that "now is the opportunity for men with aspirations to enlist in the Second Regiment. While it will be no disgrace to be drafted, the men who are will be cheating themselves of an opportunity to get in out of the draft by joining the Second Regiment. The men who are drafted won't be congratulated on the street by friends; to the contrary they will be considered somewhat shaky and uncertain." Starr, who became one of several "fighting parsons" from the Elm City, reiterated the message by saying he wished he could be chaplain of the regiment, in light of the fact that, according to one newspaper, it "has often been tried and never found waning." The Second Regiment was the pride of New Haven.

The recruitment events around the city for the 2nd Regiment—at the Bijou, Orpheum, Olympia and Shubert Theaters, at post offices and in parks—were successful to some degree. According to one source, sixteen men enlisted, thereby gaining the "opportunity of securing a special position"—everyone from that time on would enter as a private. Men were also promised that if groups enlisted together from factories or neighborhoods, they would stay together in the same regiments and perhaps even in the same companies. (This practice was well established in Britain, with regiments who often attended the same schools and lived in the same neighborhoods, kept together. It would also play out in New Haven when a group of men from Fair Haven became part of Company C of the 102nd discussed in chapter 7.) At another event on the green, Sergeant Bakewell aimed his remarks at the young women in the crowd, shouting, "You young women, what are you going to bid your sweethearts to be at this time, cowards or brave men?" The speakers promised that the 2nd Regiment would be among the first to go to France, which turned out to be true. But it was not going to be enough. Europeans had been fighting a vicious war for two years already, and newsprint and short news films made everyone aware of how awful the carnage was. Men did enlist, some after hearing rousing speeches on the green or in city parks and some after being called "yellow," as one member of the 2nd Regiment, Joe Hall, yelled at a "sturdy male passer-by." It was not enough. Soon, Congress passed the Selective Service Act, instituting a draft. The 2nd Regiment, which operated a small recruiting station next to Poli's Theater in an empty storefront—a volunteer organization for its whole history—now needed the draft.

President Wilson made clear his intent to enlist 70,000 American men between the ages of eighteen and forty in support of bringing the army to war strength. State governors were expected to facilitate this process, and

Remember, boys, you are not drafted…you are selected men.

—Representative George Gunn from Milford, at the first departure of draftees from New Haven, 1917

in 1917, Governor Marcus Holcomb of Connecticut instituted the draft for the state, the first of many. Based on population counts, in New Haven, nearly 19,000 men were required to register for the Selective Service. One June 5, 1917, the chamber of commerce building on Chapel Street hosted registration, as did the city's six designated draft boards. In the newspaper, these registrants were called "The Flower of City's Manhood"—all except for Ralph Dahlberg of 337 Central Avenue in Westville, who claimed exemption as a conscientious objector. In person, 18,547 males registered, and more than 500 sent in their registrations via mail. The City of New Haven employed 300 registrars to record the names and addresses of the men. Manufacturers and other businesses were asked by the city to send in the names of their male employees of conscription age so that names could be checked and cross-referenced. The city wanted to ensure that all men of selected service eligibility were identified. A list of all names was posted in city hall by chief registrar and city clerk A. Oswald Pallman. There was a second day to register provided to men who missed the first call. This last day was an "opportunity given them by the government to retrieve themselves from the punishment to be meted out to those who fail to obey the provisions of the draft law." Another 100 men appeared. New Haven and surrounding towns described registration day as "orderly and heavy [in terms of numbers]."

The final number for New Haven registrants for Selective Service was 20,654. Out of this number, 8,450 claimed exemption from service, mostly due to having dependents, although there were also some with "occupational diseases" and a few more with "physical unfitness." Another man living on View Street refused to register—seemingly because of a technicality. One man, Bartholomew Sevarty of 23 Downs Street, was married with a dependent, but he did not file his claim correctly and was therefore included in the first draft and "duly certified." He was quoted in the newspaper, saying, "I'm as game as the next one…and I am going up there. I wouldn't care if it wasn't for the wife and kid. I served as a member of D Company in the Second Regiment, but what is the use of talking now? I am going and never mind what I have to leave behind me, you can write it down that I am not going to quit." In other cities, men who

State of Connecticut

BY HIS EXCELLENCY

MARCUS H. HOLCOMB

GOVERNOR

A Proclamation

ONCE more are our people called upon to give a practical demonstration of democracy by the application of the selective draft in War. The principle that all should serve who share lies at the foundation of all free government. Seldom in our history has the fitness of the American people to govern themselves been better demonstrated than by the promptness, orderliness, honesty and good will with which our young men from 21 to 31 years of age complied with the provisions of the first draft.

Our men from 18 to 45, not included in the previous draft, are now about to be called upon to face a like duty and give a similar exhibition of patriotism and self-government. As the Governor of the State of Connecticut I call upon all citizens thus affected, together with their relatives and friends, to bear in mind the high traditions of this commonwealth and add new lustre to its proud name, by the fidelity and good spirit with which this federal statute is obeyed.

Given under my hand and seal of the State at the Capitol, in Hartford, this third day of September, in the year of our Lord one thousand nine hundred and eighteen, and of the independence of the United States the one hundred and forty-third.

M H Holcomb

By His Excellency's Command:

Frederick L. Perry

Secretary.

Left: Proclamation for the Selective Service (draft) issued by the State of Connecticut and Governor Marcus H. Holcomb, September 3, 1918. *Courtesy of the Connecticut State Library.*

Below: Secretary of War Newton D. Baker drawing the first number in the army draft, from the *Illustrated Memoir of the World War*. Each man registered for the selective service and duly certified would be assigned a number. These numbers were used to fill quotas established by the federal government. "Draft machinery" in Washington, D.C., selected men solely by number. The names of New Haveners with their addresses were published in the city's newspapers. On July 26, 1917, hundreds of names, addresses and draft numbers were printed in the *New Haven Register*. *Courtesy of the Yale University Library.*

refused to register were often registered by city government, "in spite of themselves." In New Haven, it was noted that city government would not "go out of their paths to round up delinquents." The names of the first six New Haven men called in the draft were published in the newspaper. As the city is divided into districts and wards, the first name called from each district was published: Arthur Rosemar of 9 Stevens Street (first district), Edward J. Stanford of 160 State Street (second district), Frederick Coombs of 81 South Water Street (third district), Raymond Curry of 179 Cove Street (fourth district), Emanuel Maurice Thalheimer of 125 Thomas Street, West Haven (fifth district) and Granville Joseph Finor of 69 Henry Street (sixth district). David Fitzgerald, the draft chairman of the third district, would become the city's mayor in 1918.

Drafted men began leaving the Elm City in the first few days of September 1917 and continued leaving in waves through the rest of the month and into October, November and December. One newspaper reported that the city's first brothers to enlist were Patrick and Barnard McGovern of 281 Ashmun Street—the same street on which Charles Henry Barclay lived. The following year would bring more quotas to fill: between two hundred and three hundred men in the early months of 1918 and then more than three hundred men in each of the summer months. Each time groups of men gathered to leave, people turned out, often in the hundreds. At the beginning, crowds gathered first on the green, from which the soldiers marched to Union Station from Elm Street, College Street, Chapel Street and State Street. One of the early trains carrying men headed to Camp Greenleaf in Georgia, and the scene they left behind—of "mothers, sisters and sweethearts"—was described in one paper as "most pathetic." Police and guards were used to keep the women back from the train so that it could depart on time. Most of the other days were described as "very quiet," with only small groups of relatives and close friends of "selected men" attending. One newspaper reported that Michael Flaherty, a sixty-six-year-old veteran of the Civil War who lived at 221 Howard Avenue, said goodbye to his son Christopher and "sent him forth with a smile and a blessing." Draftees were headed to one of the thirty-two cantonments established around the country and National Guard training camps. The men were headed for various branches of the armed service and different units and regiments. The variety of branches, divisions and regiments New Haveners served under is noted in chapter 10 on the Memorial Roll—Elm City residents served in the navy, the army, the ambulance corps and in the air. But many city residents were already attached to the 2nd Regiment, now part of the 102nd Regiment of the

Mayor Samuel Campner speaking to departing soldiers at a farewell parade on the New Haven Green, September 1917. *Courtesy of Robert S. Greenberg, Made in New Haven.*

Yankee Division. These enlistees and draftees went first to Camp Devens in Massachusetts for initial processing and then were returned to New Haven to integrate into Camp Yale.

Called "one of New Haven's greatest assets," the 2nd Regiment of Connecticut, based in the Elm City, was a long-standing militia unit dating to the American Revolutionary War. On August 21, 1917, the 2nd Regiment was combined with the 1st Regiment, based in Hartford, which was already in training at Goodwin Park. Colonel Ernest L. Isbell (the first commander of the 102nd—Henry "Machine Gun" Parker would be the next, see page 118) then had to make the decision of where to set up camp for the newly combined regiment of 4,500 men. In New Haven, locales identified for the training and growth of the 2nd Regiment included the F.F. Brewster estate in Whitneyville, which New Haveners know today as Edgerton Park, or the site that was eventually chosen, the grounds next to the Yale Bowl (constructed in 1914), on the west side of the city. The 102nd Infantry Regiment—there was also a 102nd Machine Gun Battalion and a 102nd Field Artillery Light Regiment, which trained at different camps—was supplemented with 50 volunteers from the 1st Vermont and 100 men from the 6th Massachusetts. The 101st, 102nd, 103rd and 104th were regiments of the 26th Division, called the Yankee Division, since most of the soldiers came from Rhode Island, Massachusetts, Vermont and Connecticut. All were National Guard of New England volunteers. The division was called into service on July 25, 1917, and mobilized at Framingham, Worcester, Massachusetts and at other camps, including Camp Yale, with a total of 27,468 soldiers by the end of the war and 958 officers. Although absorbed into the regular army, the division would always maintain a "National Guard spirit," different from the regulars. This difference is evident in the second stanza of a poem titled "National Guard" typed by Philip H. English, a New Havener attached to Company F (later M) of the 102nd, into his World War I diary:

Didn't get bars on their shoulders,
Or three months to see if they could;
Didn't get classed with the reg'lars
Or told they were equally good.
Just got a job and got busy,
Awkward they were, but intent,
Filing no claim for exemption,
Order said "Go"—and they went.

Camp Yale, a small, self-sustaining "city of tents," comprised twelve lettered companies, divided into three battalions: a machine gun company, a supply company and a headquarters company. New Havener and lieutenant Philip H. English, a motorcycle dispatch rider with Company F, transferred to Company M, called Camp Yale, the "best home the 102nd Inf. ever had." Here, soldiers drilled, ate, dug trenches, smoked, marched, joked around and slept during the summer of 1917. Timothy "Timmy" Ahearn, a first-generation Irish American who lived at 293 Poplar Street with his parents in Fair Haven, was assigned to Company C of the 102nd and stated on his State of Connecticut Military Service Record that the primary effect of the "camp experiences" he brought home was "better physical condition." No doubt trench digging had something to do with that. Various activities took place during the summer of 1917, making Camp Yale an active place. J.C. LaVin, manager of the Hotel Taft, built an "automobile field kitchen" onto a Model A (and later a Model B), intended to feed a battalion of 1,200 soldiers. LaVin tested his idea for two weeks at Camp Yale and later headed to Washington, D.C. But all was not work for the 102nd. The Girls Patriotic League, with a membership of thousands of young women from New Haven, erected two tents at Yale field during the summer of 1917, and several evenings every week, the young women hosted "dances for the soldier boys." In the June 23, 1918 issue of the *New Haven Register*, the paper reported that these were the very first recreation tents put up in American camps. Once the 102nd moved on to France, the league held weekly dances at the Lawn Club, inviting soldiers traveling through the city to attend.

The 102nd wasn't fully sequestered at Camp Yale, at the far edge of the city. The New Haven Green, called "the famous old square" and "this quaint old Green, one of the most charming features of the city" in a *New Haven Register* article from 1917, has a long tradition as a drilling site for militia men. As the *Register* stated in the December 9, 1917 issue, "[F]or the second time in memory of the present day, the central green has become the drill ground for the city. And for the second time Yale is taking a big part in this work." As far back as the seventeenth century, the green was the site of the city's three iron cannons. In the eighteenth century, the 2nd Company, Governor's Foot Guards marched here—led by its first captain, Benedict Arnold, and in the nineteenth century, the Blues and the Grays (the precursor to the 2nd Regiment) prepared to participate in the Civil War. So, when in 1917 the 102nd Regiment used the green for drills and marches, it was a continuation of a long tradition in Elm City history. Several tents were put up on the green to "inspire the people of the city with an appreciation of the fact that

Camp Yale, summer 1917. *Courtesy of the Connecticut State Library.*

Drills in the trenches at Camp Yale, summer 1917. *Courtesy of the Whitney Library, New Haven Museum.*

Soldiers drilling on the New Haven Green, circa 1917. *Courtesy of Robert S. Greenberg, Made in New Haven.*

the men of the nation were being called to its defense." The soldiers on the New Haven Green did not use real weapons (only wooden fakes). One New Haven journalist described the scene in detail:

> *Over in the corner, near the County Court House for example, you will see 50 young men spread out in open ranks, with plenty of leg and arm room between them. As you watch them lunge in unison, step back, parry and counter. You wonder a bit if it can be a gathering of young pugilists who are being taught some of the finer points of the fighting game. A little way from them another group of men are busily engaged in what seems to be some new tango step. They spring this way and that way, dip, bend and do all manner of things. One cannot help but wonder at the unison with which they perform. Suddenly, they assume the crouching attitude that one used to associate with rush line of the old football team. They move forward, to one side, up on their feet, back into crouching position and so on and so on. This is the thing that they did not used to do in the olden days when the Central Green was another sort of a drill ground. It is the modern method of training the body as well as the mind of the boy to become a thorough soldier.*

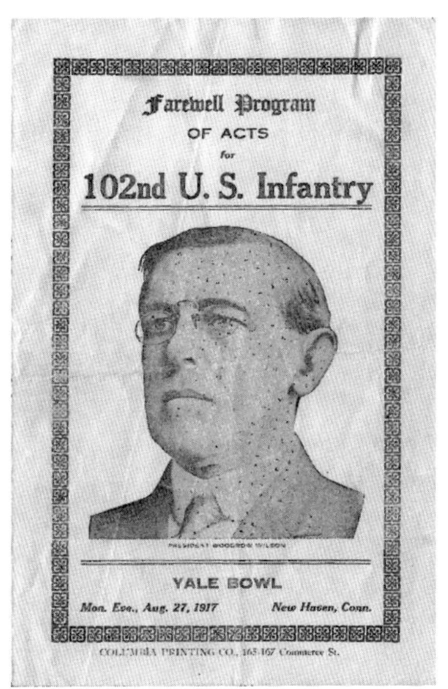

Program, Farewell Acts of the U.S. Infantry, Yale Bowl, August 27, 1917. The Yale Bowl was commonly used by the City of New Haven and Yale University for large events, but this may have been the first public spectacle lit by electricity, which drew people from across the state. The event was described as a "great outdoor carnival…a perfect fairyland of electricity" turning the darkness of the Yale Bowl's walls into "something that New Haven has never seen before." A seven-act vaudeville show was followed by the military band and the singing of "The Star-Spangled Banner." Fifty thousand people attended. *Courtesy of the Connecticut State Library.*

In the first few days of September 1917, the first men to leave New Haven for Europe and unknown experiences were Frederick K. Alling, Robert Leo, Louis Malomet, Samuel Ellsberg, William P. Sullivan, Harry E. Birney (who became a prisoner of war in a German war camp after the Battle of Seicheprey), Charles Ingoldsby, Paul Carpenter, Thomas F. Andrews, Robert A. Cooper and John Otto Frankfurter. On the order of Mayor Samuel Campner, the New Haven Red Cross provided lunches to the new conscripts, who left New Haven for Camp Devens in Ayer, Massachusetts, via Springfield. The enlistees were accompanied by Judge Cleaveland, who reported back via telegraph to the Elm City that "the comfort bags furnished by the New Haven Red Cross were greatly appreciated and the sandwiches ordered by Mayor Campner were consumed with relish on the journey." The comfort bags contained the following items: a pad, envelopes, postal cards, a shaving stick, a blue handkerchief, a tube of toothpaste, a corncob pipe, a metal box containing soap, sheep shoestrings, a housewife (sewing kit in a pouch), a bag of tobacco, a pencil, a toothbrush and a comb. When giving out the bags, Colonel Isaac Ullman said, "We hope to have other ways of reminding you boys of New Haven wherever you are." In addition, the City of New Haven gave each "selected" man cigarettes and a metal trench mirror inscribed with the words "Good Luck—New Haven."

3

SERGEANT STUBBY

New Haven Street Dog to "Great Spirit of the 26th"

At the Brook Gate entrance to London's Hyde Park, not far from Speakers' Corner, sits a war monument of a different sort: the Animals in War Memorial, erected in 2004 and dedicated to a huge array of animals. By some estimates, some sixteen million donkeys, elephants, pigeons, rats, dogs and camels served the Allies in wartime. The curved wall of Portland stone (the same material from which the chapel at Brookwood American Military Cemetery was built) is split in two, through which a horse laden with wagon wheels and a donkey prepare to enter. On the other side of the monument, another horse and a dog have already passed through the crevice. Some animals made it through the war, but as the memorial demonstrates, most did not. More than nine million died in service. Many of the horses, for example, who survived World War I were left behind and killed—once their usefulness was complete—or sold to work on farms and in quarries. Today, after one hundred years, we know more about the sentience and intelligence of all animals, and this memorial attempts to pay homage, especially in light of the fact that—as the memorial states in large letters on its façade—"They had no choice."

At the base of the memorial, on its eastern side, is laid a poppy-decorated dog collar, multiple poppy wreaths and a thick binder filled with drawings, poems and notes created by English schoolchildren dedicated to the many animals who served in World War I. Not surprisingly, among the many pages of plastic-covered drawings of all sorts of animals in war is a picture of a brown-and-white dog with pointy ears wearing a green coat with medals.

J. Robert Conroy and Stubby, March 1919. Conroy likely had the stamped *carte-de-visite* taken in France just before his return to "Yankeeland" with Stubby. Stubby is said to be the only dog who traveled across the Atlantic, served with a combat division, was wounded and returned home with the same regiment during World War I. Stubby wears his chamois coat with two service stripes—matched by Conroy's two stripes on his left sleeve—but does not yet have the plethora of medals and decorations he would receive, many after wartime. *Courtesy of Military History, National Museum of American History, Smithsonian Institution.*

Animals in War Memorial, David Backhouse, marble and bronze, Hyde Park, London, 2004. *Photograph by the author.*

The picture is of Sergeant Stubby—the most decorated animal of World War I. Seen on the opposite page is *War Horse*, the play (and later film) of the same title, an English story about the relationship between a boy and his horse. Sergeant Stubby is an American story about the relationship between a young man and his dog. And it is a true story from World War I that begins in New Haven.

Stubby is about to go to the big screen—an animated film about him and J. Robert Conroy, the Connecticut doughboy who became his best friend, will hit movie screens in 2018. Many already know the basic outline of his story, thanks to books such as Anne Bausman's *Sergeant Stubby, How a Stray Dog and His Best Friend Helped Win World War I and Heal a Nation* (National Geographic Society, 2014) and the fact that millions of visitors see him "in person" every year in the National Museum of American History's exhibit "The Price of Freedom, Americans at War." In the Smithsonian exhibit, he stands near Cher Ami, the famous carrier pigeon (whose drawing also appears with Stubby in the dedicatory booklet at the Animals in War Memorial). This taxidermy-like reminder (after death, Stubby's skin was fitted over a

Animals in War Memorial dedicatory book created by English schoolchildren, circa 2004. Sergeant Stubby at left and *War Horse* at the right. *Photograph by the author.*

plaster cast containing his ashes, earning him the name "Stuffy") does little to convey the tremendous experiences of this "ordinary tramp mongrel," as one newspaper described him—traveling overseas with "Bob" Conroy and the 102nd Regiment and participating in every battle of the Yankee Division, including the Marne, Aisne-Marne, Saint Mihiel and Meuse-Argonne. He was wounded at Seicheprey and even gassed. Three artifacts from his life—a chamois jacket hand-made for him during the war decorated with thirty patches and medals, his equally decorated harness and a portrait of him painted the year before his death—tell the story visually.

Stubby was only one animal in millions that served, but he was unique. Although many soldiers developed close relationships to their wartime service animals (some British soldiers, for example, went so far as to shoot their horses when forced to leave them behind to a life of unrelenting work in Egypt and Palestine at the end of the war), Stubby's role developed from boy and dog, to dog and regiment and, finally, to dog and division. Stubby was so popular that he became the mascot of 26th Yankee Division and even, as the cover to Conroy's scrapbook shows, the AEF mascot. The

We'll take anything for a trench companion, but, give us a dog first.

—Lieutenant Ralph Kynoch, Gordon Highlanders, quoted in the New York Herald

reasons for this can be found in any number of photographs of him—and there are many, showing him with Corporal Conroy and other soldiers in France and after the war, leading parades and participating in innumerable veteran gatherings. In these photos, it is clear this dog had a sensibility about him that traveled beyond the standard traits or divisions of species, even for the dog, known as "man's best friend." Stubby probably licked his bum and rolled in the dirt like dogs do, but he was capable of smelling "insidious vapors" (gas), alerting the troops on the western front, marching in parades "in perfect alignment and with his head held erect as though he realized his responsibility" (without a lead and sometimes with a small American flag standing straight up, attached to the coat on his back) and posing with the utmost poise for photographs and paintings. Although one angry retired soldier complained in the newspaper that Stubby had done "nothing, absolutely nothing, but sneak along behind his master and wonder what the hell was going on," the soldier missed the point: during wartime, Stubby brought companionship and cheer to a situation characterized by one newspaper as "fields of gore." The soldier, writing from San Antonio, Texas, criticized the medals and awards given to Stubby—and the moniker "hero war dog"—but the decorations given to Stubby were not only a sign of humanity's need to find something good in the middle of the bad but also of the cultural practice of commemoration. In this way, World War I was very much part of the nineteenth century, an era of stratified social formality in which political, military, religious and other designations were codified and celebrated in decorations such as artist-designed medals.

Stubby did not receive any special training—he was found walking around Camp Yale, the training grounds of the 102nd Regiment, when Conroy met him, perhaps both attracted to the camp kitchen—but his intelligence, captured by artist Charles Ayer Whipple (1859–1928) in this portrait in 1925, is clear. Here Stubby stands, looking straight at the viewer, clipped ears slightly back, his jowly neck beginning to hang a bit, his brown-and-white brindle coat less pronounced, his black nose shaped as a double curl and his "four paws that carried him over the battlefields of France" resting on the table, which Whipple has painted out of the

Stubby, Cher Ami and other materials used by Americans in World War I displayed in "The Price of Freedom, Americans at War" permanent exhibit, National Museum of American History, Smithsonian Institution, Washington, D.C. *Photograph by the author.*

scene. Stubby is very much a sentient being, that is, a living creature who thinks and feels—and even smiles. As photographs show, Stubby's wide jaws would open at the hinge into an incredibly wide black-rimmed smile, with his broad tongue curling up at the end. Although the Animals in War Memorial is right to suggest that most animals who entered service during World War I had no choice, this was not true for Stubby. He wanted to go with Conroy, and go he did, first smuggled across the Atlantic in Conroy's jacket and later, his fame growing, as a commissioned sergeant in the 102nd Regiment, Yankee Division. Sergeant Stubby wore dog tags imprinted with a number like any other soldier.

More is known about Stubby than about Whipple himself. In the September 11, 1897 issue of the *Illustrated American*, Whipple is called "A Popular Painter of American Public Men." And, in fact, he was a popular painter of public men, creating dozens of portraits between the last decade of the nineteenth century and the first two decades of the twentieth century. Although he was a prolific painter (much like an earlier version of New Haven's Deane Keller, whose portraits of public men in the Elm City appear in almost every public building), little has been written about Whipple in art historical scholarship. This is unusual considering that Whipple, originally from Boston and New York, worked for many years in Washington, D.C., opening a studio there and repainting sections of the Brumidi Corridor in the Capitol. He was known, in fact, as the "Artist of the Capitol." Here in D.C. it is likely Whipple came into contact with Conroy and Stubby, who were also in the city at the time. Conroy attended

Portrait of Stubby, Charles Ayer Whipple, oil paint on canvas, 1925. *Courtesy of the West Haven Veterans Museum & Learning Center.*

Stubby is home again. According to his owner, Stubby is in favor of some kind of League of Nations for he doesn't want the dogs of war loose in the world again. He prefers home.

—Special to the Courant, *April 7, 1919*

Georgetown University and worked in the city after the war. By the time Stubby sat for Whipple, the dog was coming close to the end of his life and "enter[ed] Valhalla," as the *New York Times* reported, the following year on March 16, 1926. Unfortunately, the record seems to be nonexistent about how the commission came about. (Who was the painting for? Conroy or Whipple himself or someone else?) Whipple died in 1928. In viewing some known portraits by Whipple, such as copies of portraits of Benjamin Franklin and Ulysses S. Grant, several of admirals and governors, the official portrait of President McKinley in the National Portrait Gallery and even animal pictures, such as a painting of a long-haired black cat with a red bow, it is clear that his portrait of Stubby reached a level of competence and spirit that many if not most of Whipple's other works of art did not achieve. This statement is supported by the fact that Whipple's artwork, including a panel called the *Spirit of 1917*, was removed from the Brumidi Corridors in the 1990s during conservation and restoration. His work was seen as fouling the original work by Constantino Brumidi, the original painter of the Capitol. This, combined with the fact that art history has forgotten him, leads to the conclusion that although he successfully ran a studio in New York City and Washington and received many commissions, Whipple's work has not stood the test of time. In my view, the portrait of Stubby redeems him.

Animals portraits were not new. English painters, such as George Stubbs, created huge canvases of horses and exotic animals in the eighteenth century, so it is no surprise that works of fine art were done of Stubby, especially considering his great fame. While the portrait of Stubby captures the spirit and intelligence of the dog, the painting also documents the amazing artifact Stubby wore on his back from 1917 until his death—his chamois coat, sewn for him by "nearly a hundred French demoiselles" in Château-Thierry, France, during wartime. The coat fit around Stubby's neck and fastened at the chest with a button and a loop and also closed under his ribcage and belly with another set of metal snap closures. On both sides of the coat were pinned various medals and decorative pins, and on the left side, the name "Stubby" was sewn in cord. Also sewn with cord under the medals are the words "102nd

US INF." Over Stubby's rump was sewn a large roundel "Victory" patch, with the waving flags of the Allies embedded in a laurel wreath, the ancient and traditional symbol of the victorious. In the photograph, it is possible to see a piece of black cord that has been cut, hanging from the Victory patch—this was where an Iron Cross hung, resting on Stubby's lower back, right above his stubbed tail. Somewhere along the way, the Iron Cross—the German military decoration for bravery—disappeared, but due to historic photographs and the painting, we know Stubby wore one. There are conflicting stories about how Stubby obtained the Iron Cross. One newspaper story says that the dog "picked up [the medal] while foraging in No Man's Land," while another says Stubby captured a German lost in the maze of bushes and tree clumps and thus "to the victor went the spoils." Another object that has gone missing is a large, solid silver medal awarded by the Eastern Dog Club of Boston. Stubby wore this medal on his chest and it appears in some photographs, but its location today is unknown.

The following is a list of the medals, badges and buttons of various kinds that Stubby collected over the course of almost ten years with Conroy,

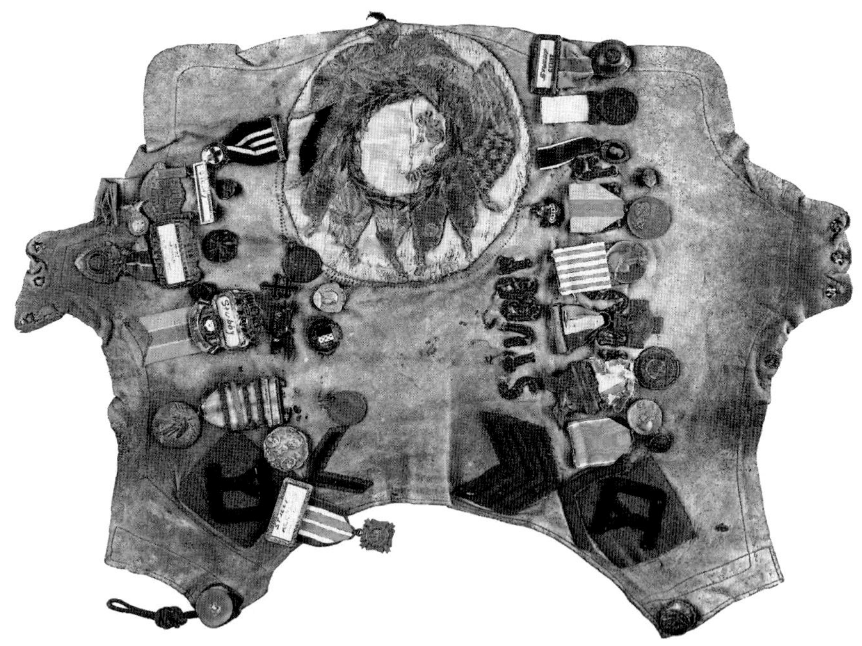

Stubby's coat, chamois, hand-made in France, circa 1917. *Courtesy of Military History, National Museum of American History, Smithsonian Institution.*

Stubby only a dog? Nonsense! Stubby was the concentration of all we like in human beings and lacked everything we dislike in them. Stubby was the visible incarnation of the great spirit that hovered over the 26th.

—New Britain Herald, *1926*

some on western front and others on the homefront. Author Ann Bausum compiled this list, with the assistance of Kathy Golden, the associate curator of the Division of Military History and Diplomacy at the Smithsonian, who watches over Stubby's material remains. It is worth the space to reprint the list in full here because from this list it is possible to imagine the many miles Conroy and Stubby traveled with the 102nd Regiment of the 26th Division, and how his popularity continued after the war until his death in 1926. The 1920s and 1930s were busy years for remembering World War I. Annual veterans' gatherings, yearly memorial events and the design and installation of monuments and memorials across the United States (discussed in Chapter 9) ensured that World War I veterans—including Stubby—were not forgotten. Conroy and Stubby participated in many of these events, with Stubby often at the head of the parade, and in a highlight seemingly for both owner and dog—both are smiling—receiving a Humane Education Society medal from General John "Black Jack" Pershing himself on July 6, 1921, who said dogs were "man's best friend in peace or war." The next day, Stubby made the cover of the *New York Times*.

Left flank, head to tail:
Three-bar service stripe (equals eighteen months of service)
Red honorable discharge stripe
26th Yankee Division patch
Verdun medal
General Service button (25-ligne, one of four examples)
American Legion red, white and blue ribbon from Minneapolis
New Haven WWI veterans' medal. On reverse: "To her sons who went forth to war that their homes might remain at peace, 1917–1919" [for a closer look, see page 165]
French commemorative medal: Republique Française Grand Guerre, *1914–1918*
Lindsay Canadian Medal
Saint Mihiel medal
Purple Heart

Stubby and Louise Johnson, Animal Rescue League Parade, May 1921. In this photograph the American flag that Stubby wore while parading can be seen. The flag was attached to his harness and stood straight in the air. Johnson was the daughter of Colonel Johnson, of the general army staff. The parade featured Laddie Boy, President Warren G. Harding's Airdale, along with seventy-five dogs and forty horses, plus Stubby. *Photograph by Harris Ewing, Library of Congress.*

Château-Thierry medal
American Legion medal, St. Paul, Minnesota

Right Flank, head to tail:
Foreign Service/American Red Cross medal
General Service Button 25-ligne
American Legion badge, New Orleans
Maréchal Foch medal (Foch was the French army commander)
Chatillon medal (French village)
American Legion badge, Kansas City
Joan d'Arc Medal/Jeanne 1412–1431 d'Arc
Crest from Brest, France
Blue Cross of Lorraine
Ste. Genevieve pin
General Services button
American Legion badge, Omaha

Verdun medal, 21 Fevier 1916
US WWI Victory medal with five cross bars (denoting battlefield service) for:
Champagne-Marne
Aisne-Marne
Saint Mihiel
Meuse-Argonne
Defensive Sector
Humane Society medal (awarded by Pershing in 1921)
Wound stripe (Stubby was wounded by a shell fragment in April 1918 at Seicheprey and reportedly spent several weeks recovering in Red Cross hospital.)
26th Yankee Division patch
VFW badge

The length to which Americans and Europeans went in commemorating special events, places and people is evident in the "bling" that Stubby wore on his coat, but there is more still. In a photograph of Stubby in a Humane Education Society parade with Louise Johnson on May 13, 1921 (likely the same event at which he earned his medal from Pershing), Stubby wears a leather harness decorated with metal plates and cartouches, each one inscribed with places he had served or visited. The leather harness served to keep the chamois coat in place, but it also provided another surface onto which Conroy could record Stubby's exploits for all to see. For our purposes, the most evocative inscription is the cartouche placed front and center, which would have rested on his chest. Surrounded by inscriptions such as "Paris," "Chemin des Dames" and "Meuse-Argonne," the center plate reads, "Stubby, Mascot Yankee Division New Haven, Conn. to France 1917–1919." Still attached to the harness is the heart-shaped dog tax tag, from D.C., dated 1925–1926,

Stubby's harness, made in the United States, post–World War I. *Courtesy of the Military History, National Museum of American History, Smithsonian Institution. Photograph by the author.*

the last year of Stubby's life. Very much like the story of Gilbert Nelson Jerome, preserved in scrapbooks by his mother and sister, J. Robert Conroy, an Irish American doughboy from New Britain, Connecticut, saved as many memories as he could of his best friend. Stubby's chamois coat, dog tags, harness and studded collar were all donated to the Smithsonian Institution in 1954—"his Arlington" according to a few newspapers. Conroy himself lived until 1987 but never owned another dog. And, like Gilbert Nelson Jerome who wrote poetry and became the subject of the same, so, too, did Stubby. This poem was written by Sergeant John J. Curtin, who was grateful that Stubby had warned him of a gas attack in the Toul sector in 1918. Both he and Stubby were exposed (Stubby had been given a gas mask, but it didn't fit) but recovered. Curtin was said to have written this poem, "Our Regimental Mascot," and pasted it to the inside of his helmet.

Listen to me and I will tell,
Of a dog who went all through hell,
With the 102nd infantry, U.S.A.,
"Stubby" was with us, night and day.

He was smuggled across the sea,
And, certainly was full of glee,
When he landed at St. Nazaire,
He and Bob were a happy pair.

Near Neufchateau he stayed a while,
And in hiking, covered many a mile,
Then in February we left for the front,
And "Stubby" was ready to do his stunt.

A month and a half on Chemin des Dames,
"Stubby" behaved just like a lamb,
Then he went to Beaumont, in Toul,
And "Stubby" showed he was no fool.

He always knew when to duck the shells,
And buried his nose at the first gas smells,
But once a small fragment stuck in his breast,
Slightly wounded in action, was "Stubby" blessed.

He went all through Chateau Thierry drive,
And came out of it very much alive,
Then to St. Mihiel "Stubby" came,
And helped those Germans from the plain.

North of Verdun were our hardest battles,
And many men gave death rattles,
But "Stubby" came through hell O.K.,
And it ready to go back to the U.S.A.

He is a fighting bulldog of the old Y.D.,
And is the pride and joy of our company,
When we take him back to the U.S.A.,
"Stubby" will hold the stage night and day.

His owner Bob will take him home,
And nevermore will "Stubby" roam,
He'll enjoy a much earned rest,
In the place we all love best.

4

FARMS, FOOD, FITNESS, FACTORIES AND THE FLU

In 1917, when the United States declared war on Germany and the Austro-Hungarian Empire, town and gown worked together in ways never before seen. Spaces that were divided between the communities of the college town—by then a tenuous relationship two hundred years old—were opened and utilized by groups of men, women and children working in various capacities to support the war effort. New Haven's homefront was a hum of activity centered on locally led campaigns for food, books, coal, medical supplies, clothing and, as always, funds. The opportunities—and the expectation—to help were clear; no one was to sit on the sidelines while New Haven soldiers marched off to war. Multiple efforts on the homefront supported soldiers on the western front, and for at least two years, 1917–19, town and gown were united. New Haven's already well-established religious, social, health and educational organizations meant that the city was poised to jump into this work quickly and with determination. The diverse programs and projects cut across gender, religion, age and ethnicity.

The city's green became training grounds for the Home Guard and army and navy recruits from Yale and the city. The university's oak-paneled dining hall became the workroom for the New Haven chapter of the American Red Cross. Yale history professor Rollin Osterweis wrote, "[I]n fact, nearly 150 women's organizations in the city were clearing their programs through the Women's Committee of the War Bureau." For men, Do Your Bit Clubs and the Four-Minute Men were established, while boys from New Haven left school after exams to become farm laborers

"Can Fruits and Vegetables and Can the Kaiser Too!" Home Canning & Drying, Victory Edition, National War Garden Commission, 1919. New Haven operated multiple canning kitchens available to anyone in the city and county at a nominal price. Managed by and mostly utilized by women, canning fruits and vegetables grown locally in war gardens was intended to supplement food on the homefront. In this image, women who participate in canning helped to defeat the "unsweetened" Kaiser, Wilhelm II of Germany. The original image was created by J. Paul Verrees in 1918 and was also the title of a popular marching song for the U.S. Army. *Courtesy of the Yale University Library.*

These are canning days in this city.

—New Haven newspaper, 1918

under the U.S. Boys Working Reserve program in order to increase the output of food production. Boy Scouts worked to collect books for the American Library Association (ALA) and sold liberty bonds while Camp Fire Girls baked and sold "war bread" on the New Haven Green. A community canning kitchen was created at Suffrage House. Walter Camp, the well-known football coach, designed a fitness program "putting the man of fifty in shape for service." The mayor's fuel committee worked to find ways to conserve coal, still a major source of fuel. The 3,200 young women of the Girls' Patriotic League pledged to work at least two hours every week on league activities. Liberty bond drives and any number of other war campaigns to raise funds, including thrift stamps from local merchants led by Shartenberg's Department Store and liberty loan drives at Poli's Palace Theater, were carried out daily.

One of the most important efforts was the national campaign for the increased production and conservation of food. The U.S. Department of Agriculture (USDA) led this campaign, which filtered down from Washington, D.C., to local communities across the United States. The USDA predicted that during the winter of 1917–18, the Allied food supplies would be strained to the point of starvation. One newspaper stated that 60 percent of factory-canned goods were requisitioned for soldiers on the western front. Those on the homefront were expected to make up the difference to keep their own families well fed. Americans were called on to reduce and conserve—especially wheat, meat, fat and sugar. The USDA expected local libraries to help in carrying out campaign work, since "no other country has issued such a wealth of publications on agriculture and home economics and placed them so generously at the command of the people." Some of the printed literature coming out of the USDA included instructions on canning, preserving and drying fruits and vegetables. A "Hoover pledge card," made into a sign, still exists in the New Haven Public Library's Local History Room. This kind of card was distributed to households by the USDA, part of promotional campaign to encourage the heads of households to engage in food conservation practices. If people filled out the card with their name and address—making a pledge to the USDA—they were entitled to receive a "Membership Window Card," which would show anyone visiting their houses that they were following the "Home Card of Instruction," or those instructions given out by the USDA for food conservation. A national campaign, in Connecticut, cards were printed in Italian, Slovakian, Polish and Hungarian in addition to English.

Increasing acreage under cultivation in New Haven County was of paramount importance in the years 1916–18. Almost twelve thousand acres of new land were cultivated between 1917 and 1918 in the war years in New Haven County, with thirty to forty thousand new growers across the state, despite the problem of severe labor shortage. One way farmers were able to increase their food production was through labor of the Boys' Working Reserve USA. Under the guidance of the Central Branch of the YMCA, boys from local public schools went out to the surrounding countryside to work on farms, thereby helping both with the labor shortage caused by men going off to war and in increasing acreage. Some two hundred boys from New Haven went to "farm camp," where they worked ten hours every day, 7:00 a.m. to 5:00 p.m., which one newspaper described as "a healthy and educating sport" for the "city boys." One farm invested in this scheme was that of A.N. Farnham and B.P. Farnam, whose farm was on Pine Rock in

PLEDGE CARD FOR UNITED STATES FOOD ADMINISTRATION

IF YOU HAVE ALREADY SIGNED, PASS THIS ON TO A FRIEND.

TO THE FOOD ADMINISTRATOR:

I am glad to join you in the service of food conservation for our nation and I hereby accept membership in the United States Food Administration, pledging myself to carry out the directions and advice of the Food Administrator in my home, insofar as my circumstances permit.

Name........

Street........

City........ State........

There are no fees or dues to be paid. The Food Administration wishes to have as members all of those actually handling food in the home.

Anyone may have the Home Card of Instruction, but only those signing pledges are entitled to Membership Window Card, which will be delivered upon receipt of the signed pledge.

Sample of pledge, which women will be asked to sign next week.

Pledge card for the U.S. Food Administration's food conservation campaign. Filling out this enrollment card entitled the member to a Membership Window Card and a Home Card of Instruction. Each head of household pledged to follow the directions of the food administrator, "insofar as…circumstances permit." *Courtesy of the Local History Room, New Haven Free Public Library.*

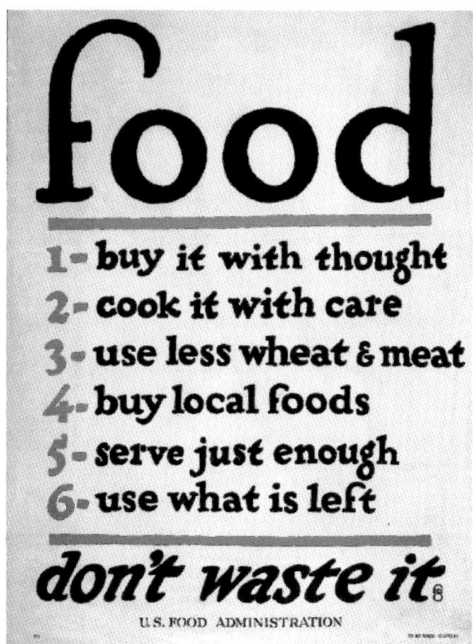

Left: "Food Save" poster, circa 1917, U.S. Food Administration. In addition to the well-known food conservation efforts around meat, wheat, sugar and fat, Americans were also saving scraps of food for unusual uses. This includes the campaign for peach "stones" (or fruit pits) collected in the lobby of the Olympia Theater and in barrels and bins around the Elm City. The peach stones were ground down to make carbon used in gas masks; two hundred pits were needed for each mask. Participating in this effort, Lovell School students were praised for their "patriotic habit of thrift." *Library of Congress.*

Right: Pin, Boys' Working Reserve U.S.A., circa 1917–18. *Library of Congress.*

Westville, in a little valley between Pine Rock and West Rock (perhaps the area of Common Ground High School today). The Farnhams, with the assistance of the YMCA, built a wooden shack to serve as a kitchen, and there was also a large tent close by with "tables and comfortable chairs, so that the boys might read, play games, or study in the evening." The boys lived in pyramid tents (much like the ones found in the 102nd Regiment camp at Yale Bowl), with wooden double deck framing that created beds. Each boy earned $1.50 a day and paid $6.00 per week for room and board ($1.00 a day, with no work on Sundays), which came out of his weekly pay.

At the Farnham farm, the boys grew onions and spent much time weeding, watering, hoeing and picking fruit and vegetables. More farms operated outside the city, such as one in the town of Orange. The Boys' Working Reserve had five camps across the United States in 1917, with Dr. Charles Kirschner, principal of New Haven High School, as one of the first camp directors. Boys were allowed to leave school for the farm camps if they "pass their exams and reach a certain high percentage," which was applied to both boys in grammar school and high school, indicating that some boys were not going to continue directly with high school. When applying for farm camp, individuals had to sign up for sixty-day stays. The scheme apparently received criticism, with some calling the plan "unfeasible," but local farmers took to the opportunity, planting more crops than they could harvest alone. At the end of their tenure, the boys were promised "badges and bars… and a certificate signed by Governor Holcomb." Farm camps were clearly modeled on army life, and the enlisted boys were "enrolled" in service, with their white pyramid tents, long workdays and badges and bar indicating length and quality of service. These young men were, in a sense, in training, should the war last longer than a year.

In 1917, seven hundred boys served across the state, and the success of the Boys' Working Reserve across the United States meant that a drive to enlarge the program was called for in 1918. Enrollment drives were undertaken in local public schools on March 18, 1918, for boys between the ages of fourteen and twenty-one for a summer's service on farms. Kirschner was named the director of the statewide program in 1918 due to the city's success, which was documented in a survey sent out by the Connecticut Agricultural College (today the University of Connecticut). The majority of the three hundred farmers responded positively to the boy farmers.

In addition to the "juvenile farms," New Haven school-age children were encouraged to participate in the food conservation movement in another way—each student brought home a pledge card (much like the ones given to their mothers) that listed foods they could raise and/or preserve. It was suggested by the Connecticut Junior Food Army (under the auspices of the State Council of Defense) that children could grow one to two acres of corn, cultivate one to eight acres of potatoes or can fifty quarts of fruit or vegetables. Children with access to land could also raise a pig, a flock of chickens or sheep. The

Food Will Decide the War

Save the Wheat
Save the Meat
Save the Fats
Save the Sugar
Save the Fuel
For Your Soldiers on the Front
Need Them All

—*U.S. Food Administration,*
World War I

April 14, 1918 issue of the *New Haven Register* reported that the Farm Bureau sponsored an egg-laying contest for young people in the city and that Lawrence Carney of 53 Audubon Street and Ruth Stephen of 137 Nicholl Street were "among the most enthusiastic." Photographs of the New Haven teenagers with their chickens and coops appeared under the headline "Economy Egg-Laying Contest Conducted by Farm Bureau Waxes Hot Among Young Folk." If a child filled out a pledge card and fulfilled that pledge, he or she would be sent a certificate of merit from the governor. At the end of the summer of 1918, an exhibit was held in Mount Carmel (today, across the line in Hamden) showcasing their efforts. The winners of the Mount Carmel agricultural fair then went on to compete at the state level. The public library also held an exhibit of items from the gardens on September 20 and 21.

In 1918, it was reported that New Haven County had raised 225 pigs, but the following year, due to the pledge drive, 800 pigs were raised—providing, according to one newspaper, the most precious food commodity of all: fat. Pigs were the central focus of the Farm Bureau. One young man named Walter Johnson, living in Northford, won the second prize for his sow Peter. Peter was not "dispatched" but continued to grow all through the winter, and then when spring came, she birthed a litter of 13, which the Farm Bureau boasted were the "finest litter of pigs in New Haven County." Pigs were not the only animals raised by New Haven students; the Junior Food Army provided one hundred ewes to boys and girls in the spring of 1918, thus growing a new class of laborer, the shepherd. The landscape of New Haven County—rocky, high land—was perfect for sheep. The Farm Bureau estimated that the raising of sheep for mutton and wool could bring in a $100,000 a year, utilizing land that was of little use to others. One bank in New Haven, First National, provided the funds to the Economy Egg Club, which in turn sponsored six city students to raise six pullets (baby chicks) each. At Strong School, four thousand students pledged to cultivate gardens, the largest number across the state, followed by Meriden and Waterbury.

As noted, the "heads of households" were expected to "put in practice new and far-reaching economies." Women were expected to can extra fruit and jellies to send to soldiers on the western front as well as produce extra food for their families. Canning fruits and vegetables became one of the most active areas for New Haven women. The State of Connecticut sponsored a "Canning Corps," with New Haven County expected to produce 350,000 quarts of fruits and vegetables (out of Connecticut's goal of 5 million). Emily

Whitney, chairman of the New Haven committee of the County Farm Bureau, opened a community canning kitchen in the "Suffrage House" at 91 Grove Street offering jars and sugar and had an expert supervisor on hand. Classes went on in all sorts of places across the Elm City, from the YWCA and churches to social organizations and even schools. Corn and tomatoes were canned in schools under the supervision of a Miss Ferguson, the emergency food agent of the County Farm Bureau. The new method of canning, called "cold-pack," was often demonstrated about the city; on August 1, 1917, a Miss Knowlton gave a demonstration of canning on the grounds between the county courthouse and the public library (today a driveway)—notable to the newspapers as the first canning class ever held outdoors. But not everyone had access to transportation, so one editorial in the local paper suggested that "some committees could devote attention to the collection of gifts."

In order to have enough fruit and vegetables to can, drives such as Connecticut's Home Garden campaign planted 65,000 new gardens in backyards and vacant lots—4,500 in New Haven County alone—with home and school gardens overseen by the Junior Ward and/or Boy Scouts. Girls, called "farmerettes," participated in farming activities, working on twelve war gardens through the Girls Patriotic League. Even the New Haven Police were called in to assist. At a New Haven Board of Aldermen meeting in the spring of 1918, a resolution was passed that "the chief of police instruct the entire police force to give particular attention to the protection of private gardens and especially the gardens of school children working on the City Farm Plan." They furthered authorized the Boy Scouts to act with the authority of the police department in the protection of city gardens. Prizes were given at public displays, such as one held at the New Haven Public Library. According to one newspaper, lectures on the war garden were given on Friday nights at the high school so that the "advice will be fresh in the minds of the schoolboys and girls on Saturday, when they have at last a half day in the garden."

The New Haven chapter of the American Red Cross opened the YMCA building on Chapel Street as a canning center for fruits and vegetables for later consumption in Red Cross hospitals. One newspaper exhorted New Haven women to become active participants in the new large-scale endeavor: "[I]n order to do this the women of the city must give some of their time in aid of the plan and while they are assisting in the canning work, they will also be receiving valuable instruction in this detail of modern domestic science." If women were not able to give their time, they were encouraged

Let the Kaiser beware this child army whose work is showing such excellent results.

—New Haven newspaper article about juvenile farmers, 1917

to donate glass jars or preserve jars, which were needed in large numbers; fruits and vegetables if there were leftovers from their own gardens; or money with which the Red Cross could purchase supplies. Sugar was also most desirable, so the wholesale and retail merchants of the city were expected to contribute in this way. The oncoming winter of 1917–18 was utilized by organizers using moralistic tones: "[F]ailure to prepare vegetables and fruit for winter use by drying is one of the worst examples of American extravagance," said one manual. New Haven County Farm Bureau, located at 185 Church Street, spearheaded the "full pantry movement," helping farmers, housewives, boys and girls in organizing a Junior Food Army. Girls in the eighth grade and high school were active canners, attending workshops along with the women of New Haven. Even the New Haven Gas Light Company held demonstrations in canning and drying under the direction of Mathilde Hawkins, director of the School of Science from the YWCA. By August 1918, all of the work done on the homefront resulted in the report that $4 million was added to the nation's "food wealth."

For both British and American breweries, the shortage of wheat was a problem in 1918. In a city and state with deep Puritan foundations, the pastors of the Nutmeg State came together to urge the creation of a "campaign of conservation to conserve wheat." Cereals such as barley are the main ingredient of brewing beer, one of the largest food industries in New Haven in the first decades of the twentieth century. During wartime, barley began to replace wheat as the ingredient in bread due to wheat shortages. Although the pastors' union claimed that they were "prompted to this communication by the insistent inquiries coming to them from members of their congregations," it is likely that religious leaders were able to use grain shortages to support their temperance efforts. Called "economic waste," the production of beer was adversely affected in Great Britain, too, during the war years. But in New Haven and other American cities, the temperance movement was gaining ground; wartime provided ammunition for "pastors and housewives"—those directly involved with the temperance movement—in their quest to limit consumption of alcoholic beverages. Sensitive to public criticism, the pastors said, "The matter is no longer one of sentiment—much less of fanaticism…[but] nothing less than

Charles Lathrop Pack, president of the National War Garden Commission, with his "army" of crops, by Jay Norwood "Ding" Darling. Pack reads the announcement, "Uncle Sam expects every war garden to do its duty." The potato wears a Civil War cap—an old soldier back at war. "Enemy plotters" appear in the form of cabbage worm, black rust and the potato bug. Published in the *New York Herald Tribune*. *Courtesy of the Connecticut State Library.*

injustice coupled with unwisdom." Brewing in New Haven, which dates to 1646, only eight years after the settlement was founded by English Puritan immigrants, stayed intact in the Elm City until Prohibition decimated the city's more than twelve breweries.

New Haven's Four-Minute Men, chaired by then-mayor Samuel Campner, "carried messages of the government to countless numbers of people of this city and the surrounding towns." The Four-Minute Men was an organization formed under the head of the Committee for Public Information, based in Washington, D.C. Woodrow Wilson was the president—both of the national organization and the country. In brief, the Four-Minute Men provided a voice for the federal government at the local level. New Haven's Four-Minute Men led campaigns to support liberty loan drives, as well as the Red Cross War Fund drive. The organization's particular method was to speak about a subject for only four minutes, hence the name. In one case, 40 speakers made 130 four-minute speeches reaching a total of 150,000 people. Apparently, New Haven's Four-Minute Men also had one female member: Isabella Feuchtwanger. Plans were put in place to start a Junior Four-Minute organization in the New Haven

Herman Sodersten, *Portrait of Samuel Campner* (1887–1934), mayor of the city of New Haven, 1917–18, 1919. Campner was born in Courland, Russia. His parents immigrated to New Haven, and Campner graduated from Yale Law School in 1908. Campner was a justice of the peace and became mayor after the death of Frank Rice—New Haven's first Jewish mayor. It is a tradition of New Haven mayors to have their portraits painted and hung in city hall at 165 Church Street after their administration ends. *Courtesy of the City of New Haven.*

public schools; according to one newspaper, by 1918, both boys and girls were already working on their four-minute speeches, much like a present-day PechaKucha presentation.

While some New Haveners joined the Four-Minute Men, another Elm City resident was organizing a group focused on fitness. Walter Camp, known today as the "Father of American Football," believed that by helping men between forty-five and sixty become more physically fit, younger men could be released from industrial jobs, enabling them to go to the front. In April 1917, Camp, then Yale University's mentor of athletics, wrote an editorial promoting his belief that a Senior Service Corps was needed to "fit older men for work that will release their juniors for the front." Already known for his football exercises, Camp wrote, "He must be handled as would the candidate for a football team, taken through a careful course of preparation, and gradually brought along the pitch of what his powers can stand." The Senior Service Corps made sure to note that it was a supplementary organization for men out of military service age. The ninety-day exercise regimen designed by Camp—a "carefully graded system of training, beginning easily and gradually working up to a condition where a march of ten miles, even with some equipment, will be possible"—occurred between 8:00 a.m. and 9:00 a.m., before the workday started. Camp's idea began in New Haven but was intended to spread to other cities and states. One New Haven newspaper said of the participants:

> *Not only can these business and professional men wield the pen, crank the auto, play golf and give verbal orders but they can shoulder and shoot a gun....Today they are soldiers where yesterday they were thinking business first, business second, and business third, business ad infinitum. Today it is some business, some soldiering, some pleasure—all which make sound health. As far as they are concerned, the home physician has been stricken off their calendar.*

New Haveners would have seen Camp and his Senior Service Corps on the green, standing at attention, going through their drills or hiking, holding metal bars as heavy as regulation guns. According to Camp's program, three-fourths of the training was in the open air. After the *New York Times Magazine* published an article about Camp in its June 24, 1917 issue, letters poured in from across the country, asking Camp for advice and guidelines for starting additional Senior Service Corps. The craze for fitness extended beyond older New Haven men—young women, members of the Girls Patriotic League, started drilling on their own using Camp's rules, going so far as to drill in the Meadow Street

Armory under the tutelage of Captain A.W. Mattoon. Fitness became a business for Camp after the end of the war. In the 1920s, he produced books, records and instruction manuals for everyone to follow his "Daily Dozen" exercises.

Although members of Camp's Senior Service Corps believed in his regimen of exercise to stave off illness, in early 1918, an influenza outbreak circled the globe, killing far more people than the war itself. Called the "Spanish flu," the virus was an exceptionally deadly strain that struck young, previously healthy adults hard (named so, due to the more than eight million people who died from the disease in Spain).

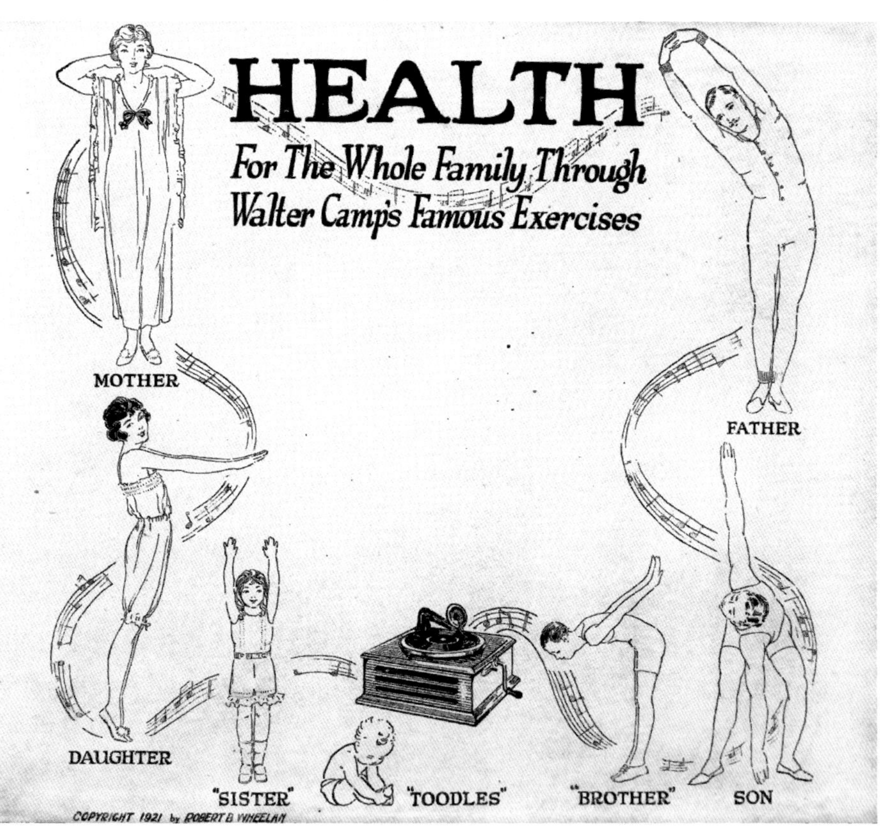

Record, "Health for the Whole Family," Walter Camp, 1921. Camp began his exercise regimen for the Yale football team but, during World War I, began applying his regimen to older men. Later, in the 1920s and 1930s, he created his "Daily Dozen" exercises for everyone regardless of gender or age. His words, "There's no substitute for hard work and effort beyond the call of duty. This is what strengthens the soul and ennobles one's character" denote his association between moral character and the physical body. *Courtesy of the Audio Preservation Fund.*

Once infected, bodies were weakened, and many were vulnerable to secondary infections such as pneumonia, often leading to death. Groups of people living in proximity—such as recruits in army camps—were especially susceptible. By the late spring, there were influenza outbreaks in fourteen of the largest army training camps on the homefront, including Fort Devens. After temporarily subsiding, a second, deadlier wave appeared in late summer. By mid-September, it had developed into a pandemic. Many servicemen caught the influenza virus in the United States and boarded troopships bound for Europe, unaware of their infected condition. Perhaps this is how Irene Flynn and Helen A. Moakley caught pneumonia; both New Haven nurses served on the western front and died of the infection in 1918, Flynn on July 13 and Moakley on August 22. The Spanish flu arrived in the city of New Haven in 1918; schools closed for two weeks, as almost one thousand people became ill and forty-three city residents died. According to one source, the average lifespan in the United States was depressed by ten years due to the infectious disease. Even Woodrow Wilson suffered from the flu during his work on the Treaty of Versailles in early 1919.

Long before influenza struck New Haven, the city's factories experienced a boom in demand that began with the war in August 1914. By 1917, newspaper articles cried out, "Work For All in War Shops of New Haven," and new training programs were geared toward unemployed men—and women. Inexperience was no longer a detriment, as "the opportunity for service offered by these manufacturers are in so many industries that there is surely a place in which each unoccupied man and woman in this city will be capable of doing something in the way of real work." Winchester Bennett, the president and treasurer of Winchester Repeating Arms Company, was selected as the munitions and equipment representative of the State Defense Council, which Governor Holcomb had put in place. Although war was not popular with the public before 1917, the Winchester Repeating Arms Company, formed in the mid-nineteenth century, began long day and night shifts in support of the war effort, receiving more than $16 million in military orders from Britain, Russia and France. By the end of 1915, the orders increased to nearly $50 million. More than nineteen thousand workers meant crowded cities and a housing shortage; the work week was expanded from the already standard fifty hours to sixty, seventy and more. Winchester was located on eighty-one acres of land, where various guns, weapons and ammunition used in the war were made, including more than 500,000 modified Enfield rifles, 27,000 Browning Automatic rifles (BAR) and 400,000 bayonets, as well as cartridge cases, service cartridges, primers and caps.

After the war, Winchester could not pay its debts and eventually shuttered during the Great Depression, only to open again during the World War II years. The problem of employment for returning soldiers was noted in the *New Haven Register*—according to one study, 80 percent of returning soldiers got their old jobs back. The remaining 20 percent, such as Timothy Ahearn of Fair Haven, did not, due to "unavoidable changes that have taken place since the boys entered the country's service." Ahearn, a clerk for Marlin Firearms Company, ended up a migrant agricultural worker. A bronze monument to him (see chapter 9) makes no note of his problematic postwar life, although several sculpture installations in the refurbished Winchester apartments—the complex is undergoing rehabilitation into

Winchester Repeating Arms Company, New Haven, circa 1917. Women were encouraged to work in New Haven's industries, which inadvertently strengthened the suffragette movement. In this image, women seem to be wearing dresses, but the wearing of trousers for certain kinds of industrial jobs helped to normalize pants for the public—which would be seen more often in Hollywood in the 1920s and 1930s. *Courtesy of the Connecticut State Library.*

Installation, Susan Clinard, Winchester Lofts, 275 Winchester Avenue, New Haven. Winchester Repeating Arms Company functioned on site until 2006, when it was shuttered for good. Clinard used "found" pieces of molds and other objects from Winchester's long manufacturing history to create several installations in the refurbished public spaces. *Photograph by the author.*

luxury lofts—remember generations of New Haveners who participated in the world wars of the twentieth century.

One last group of people should be remembered here on the homefront: those "enemy aliens" who were tied to restricted districts shown on a map of New Haven published in 1917. Enemy aliens were "not allowed within 100 yards of any munitions plant, railroad, dock, federal building or water supply." About half of the city of New Haven was kept open to resident enemy aliens, but their lives must have been turned upside down. One newspaper claimed, "[I]n spite of the fact that there has been much pressure brought to bear, to put enemy aliens in detention camps, the authorities have stuck to their original plans and have allowed considerable liberty." In addition to the scrutiny and the curtailing of their personal freedom in terms of moving around the city, several men working at Winchester were put in jail when it was discovered that they did not apply for permits issued by the U.S.

Marshal Authority under the "alien activities act." Six men were arrested, with four let go after proving they were not German citizens. Two men were kept in jail, one of whom was married in England and had four children in the Elm City. It was "not known definitely," the newspaper reported, "just how many families will be affected and seriously discommoded....[I]t is certain however, that they are to be allowed less liberty, merely as a matter of protecting the public." The experiences and the fate of these enemy aliens—called "dangerous people in the community" in New Haven—are unknown but point to problems still with us today.

5

SOLDIERS' LIBRARY SYSTEM

The New Haven Free Public Library Mobilizes

During World War I, libraries were seen not as static institutions of solitude and quiet learning but as active participants in locally led campaigns that served the war. As the USDA proclaimed of libraries, "[T]hey should be partners in all federal, state and local undertakings designed to put into practice the information contained in the publications." In other words, libraries and librarians, both on the homefront and the western front, took a leading role in efforts to reinforce city, state and federal programs at home and in supplying American soldiers with reading material—and even moral support—abroad.

As soon as cantonments and National Guard training camps were established in the summer of 1917, camp libraries were in the news, and New Haven libraries, librarians, local organizations and city residents mobilized themselves to answer the call. From their headquarters in the Library of Congress in Washington, D.C., the Library War Service of the American Library Association (ALA, still the same name today) was directed by the War Department's Commission on Training Camp Activities to guide local authorities in collecting books and magazines and getting them sorted and shipped to training camps in the United States and overseas. Called a "popular national movement" in a New Haven newspaper, in the fall of 1917, the country was asked to raise $1 million for the war library project, and by the spring of 1918, $1.6 million had been raised. In 1918, the Library War Service worked with on-the-ground organizations such as the YMCA and the Knights of Columbus to erect

The Camp Library is Yours—Read to Win the War, Charles Buckles "C.B." Falls (1874–1960), color lithographic poster, 1917. "You will find popular books for fighting men in the recreational buildings and at other points in this camp. Free. No red tape. Open every day. Good reading will help you advance. Library War Service, American Library Association." Falls, who signed his name here with a block-printed *F*, was an illustrator who designed recruitment posters during World War I. *Library of Congress.*

wood-frame buildings and staff libraries in thirty-five large camps and four hundred branch libraries—literally on the western front—and coordinated with chaplains and others to supply smaller camps with materials. In the first year, 700,000 books were sent to soldiers and sailors, though by the end of the war and the demobilization of American troops in 1919, millions of books and magazines had gone overseas.

A national fund to meet the expense of sending reading material to the front was created to alleviate more financial stress on the federal government. Cities were to contribute amounts based on size, and New Haven was listed at $8,000—or $.05 per resident—toward the shipping costs, out of the state share of $65,000 for the "million dollars for a million books for a million soldiers." Henry W. Farnham, a Yale professor, reformer and philanthropist, wrote an editorial on October 17, 1917, encouraging New Haveners to "do their bit." Farnham reported that New Haven was slow to raise the funds, corroborated by another article stating that the public's contribution "has not been what was expected....New Haven has so far lagged behind." The city had chipped in $2,000 by the fall, while other cities had already raised their full pledge. Farnham urged, "Think of five cents per capita—the price of a drink of soda water, or of a package of chewing gum, of a cigar of the cheapest grade, and even less, since the raising of the rates, than a single trolley fare!" Another newspaper reported that "few would believe that a soldier would sell part of his equipment to purchase books," employing the tactic of visual imagery to encourage action. The thought of young men in trenches willing to sell precious equipment was likely an image too gripping to ignore. Governor Holcomb considered the $65,000 sum from the state "modest" and announced that if "every man would contribute what he spent in cigars, and every woman what she expended in chocolates, the [funds] required would be easily acquired."

In addition to raising funds, cities and towns were also expected to donate books and magazines. Again, New Haven was late to the game in doing this work. By the time the Elm City started its book campaign in May 1918, Waterbury had already collected 20,000 books and Bridgeport and Hartford 30,000 each. But, in classic Connecticut competitive fashion, New Haven announced it would bring in 50,000 books by the end of 1918. The New Haven War Bureau worked with the New Haven Public Library to do this work, with women from the bureau (who were called "Minute Women," because they worked quickly—"every minute saved enables them to cover so much more territory") endeavoring to visit every house across the city to pick up wrapped packages of books. Twenty-five Boy Scouts were enlisted to help collect the books via automobile, as did Colonel North of

a million dollars
for a
million books
for a
million soldiers

—State War Library Council

BOOKS FOR U. S. SOLDIERS

Will You Help?

Dear Madam:

An organized campaign is being made in every large city, under the auspices of the American Library Association to collect a million books and magazines, which will be forwarded to army camps, the front and the hospitals. New Haven is to do her share in this splendid movement. Our young men are making great sacrifices to serve their country and need books for study, recreation, and diversion in lonely moments. There must be a few idle books in nearly every home in the city. You can "do your bit" now by gathering these together and notifying the Public Library by postal or telephone, and your contribution will be called for during the week of September 3, when an organized campaign to secure books is to be launched.

Books on the war, popular travel, history and biography, as well as short stories, detective stories, stories of the sea and adventure are especially desired, as well as current magazines.

Stirring poetry is in request—Service, Kipling, Masefield, Noyes, etc., —as well as good drama.

Books of travel and history, especially in the countries at war. Lives of heroes, great men and women, especially of famous contemporaries.

Bring a little happiness to our boys and help them forget the dangers they may encounter at any moment.

It is the sacred duty of all who remain at home to provide some comfort for our heroic defenders.

Do your part at once.

NEW HAVEN FREE PUBLIC LIBRARY

Above: Library War Service, YMCA tent, Vancouver barracks, World War I. This image from Vancouver (possibly one of the Canadian Expeditionary Force camps) shows all of the necessary pieces of a camp library, including bookshelves, a table with ink and paper and the presence of a professional librarian, keeping his eye on things. *Library of Congress.*

Left: Books for U.S. soldiers, *Will You Help?* flyer, circa 1917–18. The last two lines in bold hold the reader accountable for his or her actions: "It is the sacred duty of all who remain at home to provide some comfort for our heroic defenders. Do your part at once." The phrase "heroic defenders" was a historical touchstone for New Haven; the City of New Haven erected the Defenders Monument, dedicated to the Revolutionary War, in 1911. The bronze sculpture of the "defenders of New Haven" was well known due to newspaper coverage. *Courtesy of the Local History Room, New Haven Free Public Library.*

the Home Guard, who offered use of the organization's automobile as well as his personal car to collect books. They were joined by the New Haven Automobile Club and local theaters, clubs and fraternal organizations. The clergymen of the city were also asked to "make a definite appeal to their congregations." Students from New Haven High School, Gilbert Nelson Jerome's alma mater, went from house to house to collect books. Pershing himself had ordered that fifty tons of cargo space per month—enough room for 100,000 books—was dedicated to reading material for soldiers.

The movement to mobilize reading material had multiple purposes. First, reading was seen as a way to prevent depression on the western front and for "keeping up the moral tone of the rank and file." Officers recognized that "providing books for them to read is a large and vital contribution toward keeping them happy under the strain of trench and camp life." Another newspaper reported, "[A] good book may break the mental strain under which the soldier labors and by giving him an hour's pleasure render a most important service." Reading was also an important part of hospital recuperating time. New Haven mayor Samuel Campner was quoted in the newspapers: "[L]et us plan in every way possible for the comfort of the soldier boys and remember that one of their most constant comforts is good reading and plenty of camp libraries." Dr. Henry Van Dyke affirmed the relationship between books and morale:

> *One thing this war has certainly taught the world, and that is that victory does not depend solely upon "big battalions," but upon large and strong and brave hearts and minds in the battalions. The morale of the army is the hidden force which uses the weapons of war to the best advantage, and nothing is more important in keeping up this morale than a supply of really good reading for the men, whether they are in campaign preparing for the battle, or in the trench waiting to renew the battle again, or in the hospital wounded and trying to regain strength of body and mind to go back to the battle for which they have enlisted. Human fellowship, books, and music are three of the best tonics of the world. I believe these things very thoroughly.*

New Haveners were encouraged to donate books "on the war, popular travel, history and biography," as well as "short stories, detective stories, stories of the sea and adventure," although "any readable book of general interest will appeal to the soldiers, as there are men of varying tastes among them." City residents were also warned to not donate books that were dated: "The donors of periodicals and books have learned their lessons as to the kind of books wanted. They know that periodicals of the year 1890, books published in the last quarter of the last century, technical reports, and other volumes which are given to be gotten out of the way as useless for the purpose in hand.…Such books should be given to the ragman, not the soldier or sailor." One tongue-in-cheek article from 1918 thanked donors for sending in "school readers antedating the Civil War" and "annual reports of the Episcopal Eye and Ear Hospital." It was noted that "three-quarters of its demand of its patrons is for fiction, but in the camps this proportion is exactly reversed: that is, the soldiers take out three technical books to one of fiction."

At this time the provision and circulation of books and other reading matter among the soldiers and sailors at home and abroad makes an appeal to all friends of a righteous cause.

—Connecticut State Board of Education

For soldiers and sailors reading fiction, a list of favorite authors was published in the *Sun* on March 15, 1918. Many of the favored authors are still read far and wide today, while others are forgotten, perhaps known today only to literature scholars. The published list included O. Henry, Harold Bell Wright, Jack London, G.H. McCutcheon, Robert W. Chambers, Sir Arthur Conan Doyle, Mark Twain, E. Phillips Oppenheim, Kipling, Poe, Booth Tarkington, Rider Haggard, Dumas, H.G. Wells, Joseph Conrad and John Fox Jr. New Haven also noted that "good poetry and drama can be utilized." American soldiers, most of whom like Gilbert Nelson Jerome had never been out of the country, were also studying French while stationed on the western front, therefore French grammar books and dictionaries were requested, as were "easy readers and stories" and French "attractive magazines." Jerome, an aviator in France, wrote of his desire for reading material to his mother in November 1917:

> *These non-flying days are very dull. Time was when we used to wander over the fields to nearby villages and sketch various artistic bits, but increased restrictions prevent all this. So we mope around the barracks and kill time as we may. Wild card games and the shouts of the multitude make writing and reading difficult. Also there is little to read. A few magazines come to hand, but I hunger for a few worthwhile books. I wish Jennie would be on the lookout for something to send me. Philosophy and psychology would be welcome, or possibly something in the line of war literature.*

The Connecticut State Council of Defense helped the ALA assist local libraries. Under the methods of modern librarianship, the ALA also provided guidelines to local groups that were offering the books to soldiers and sailors, providing a rubber stamp with the "ALA War Service" initials and encouraging them to implement a system of lending that replicated methods in use in public libraries: "To lend books some sort of record is essential. Otherwise books will be lost." They instructed folks how to use a manila pocket and card system glued to the inside front cover of a book—a system still in use until the turn of the twentieth century. A bookplate glued to the inside of the book was another method encouraged by the ALA, meant to prevent loss. New Haveners were also encouraged to write their names and addresses on the inside cover of the books they donated so that "the soldier who reads it will know that someone in New Haven is his friend and stands ready to help him."

The funds raised by the city would be used to buy books and magazines, but, as reported on October 30, 1917:

> *Something more than books is needful....* [A] *lot of books, even good books, huddled together in an unattractive room, from which readers are invited to help themselves is no more a library than a delicatessen shop is a restaurant. There must be buildings for housing and caring for the books, they must*

C.B. Falls, "War Service Library" bookplate, circa 1917–18. This bookplate image replicated—on a small scale—the *Books Wanted* poster, which Falls designed for the American Library Association, along with the *Camp Library Is Yours* image. Falls received professional success from these images and became a member of the Society of Illustrators. This small bookplate—printed on thin paper—is a rare survivor of World War I and the lengths to which Americans went to supply soldiers with reading material. *Courtesy of the Local History Room, New Haven Free Public Library.*

> *be arranged, and kept in repair, and added to as the demands require; the reader must be helped to just the book he wants, and perhaps be shown how to use it to the best advantage. These things can be done only by a competent librarian, trained in the work. A good librarian is necessary to make a library effective under ordinary circumstances, but he is still more necessary in the cantonments.*

These frame buildings—one story, containing a large, open, open-shelf room surrounded by books—furnished with chairs and tables were used for "reading and reference, but [also] provided them with a table, stationary [*sic*] and writing materials, so that the soldier might find a clean, and comfortable place for writing letters home." While at Camp Devens training Connecticut soldiers, Colonel D.F. Craig, commander of the 302nd Field Artillery, said, "My men must write home. This is not a request, but a command. No soldier that fails to write home will be a good soldier." In the eyes of John Lowe, who published an editorial in the *Republican* as early as May 1917, just one month after the United States entered the war, libraries at home were becoming centers for "information and inspiration" with patriotic posters on the walls. Public libraries, whether on the homefront or the western front, were special places not to be contaminated by the recruiting process. Libraries, both home and abroad, were to be run by professionals not by "enthusiastic but ill-instructed amateurs."

After the armistice, the demand for books and periodicals was even greater. The desire was expressed by Herbert Putnam of the Library of Congress in a cablegram in 1918: "Need never greater than present for at least a million more miscellaneous books, demanded within six months to maintain army morale." One newspaper noted that there was a "remarkable change in the character of reading matter demanded by the soldiers in France and Germany…when the shells were flying over the trenches it was light fiction they wanted: books that helped them forget the whistle of shells and required little mental effort. Now there is almost no demand for fiction, and the boys are asking for books of some educational value." Books were seen by the soldiers as a way to prepare for life after war—vocational textbooks, foreign language instruction and technical

> *The people of New Haven are urged to give every book possible to this cause, as the contribution of so many people makes it one of the most patriotic efforts of the war.*
>
> —*New Haven newspaper, 1917*

Alfred A. Cohn photographed this corner of a public library showing C.B. Falls's *Books Wanted* poster. Gelatin silver print, circa 1917–18. The full caption of the poster reads, "Books wanted for our men in camp and over there. Take your books to the public library." *Library of Congress.*

surveys were all requested. And so, after the armistice, as the Allies became the Army of Occupation, library stations were set up wherever they were, including Coblenz and other cities on the Rhine in Germany.

Beyond the collection and preparation of books for soldiers in cantonments, camps and the western front, New Haven libraries and librarians were instructed to become well acquainted with all of the community programs serving the war cause, including food production and conservation, munitions manufacturing and military and naval training. In other words, libraries were expected to become centers of information for anything and everything that had to do with war both on the homefront and the western front. "Can you tell a man over the telephone how to get rid of insects on his potatoes and cabbage? If you can, you are ready to serve your country and helping to win the war" said the *War Service Library Week Bulletin*. Additionally, librarians were encouraged to gather as much material as possible available "in sufficient quantity to meet unusual demands." The *War Service Library Week Bulletin* suggested that "every librarian wants to help win the war. Here is your opportunity—right in your own profession."

Librarians were encouraged to "create demands for information and service" by holding a War Service Library Week in all the libraries in America. They were instructed to "work up your own enthusiasm; realize that this is a patriotic duty and a wonderful opportunity to make folks realize the practical value of libraries." In their efforts, librarians were expected to be "enthusiastic and aggressive." In order to do this, libraries were encouraged to "keep newspapers filled with news articles, book lists, pictures and editorials" and "have displays in store windows, banks, club rooms, public buildings, etc." in addition to putting "posters and signs both inside and outside of street cars" and "moving picture theaters." For those with a church bent, "have library sermons in all churches on Sunday preceding War Service Library Week." The "Subjects Made Prominent by the War" with which librarians were expected to be familiar included:

Business Efficiency in Wartime
(a) In production
(b) In marketing
Food Values
Wartime Transportation
Wartime Economy in the Home
Women and the War
Red Cross Work

New Haven Free Public Library Reference Room, 1926. The New Haven Free Public Library, also known as the Ives Memorial branch of the New Haven Public Library, was designed by Cass Gilbert in the Beaux-Arts style and opened in 1911. *Courtesy of the Local History Room, New Haven Free Public Library.*

Wartime Thrift
Shipbuilding
Aviation and Submarines
Military Training
Explosives, Guns and Shells
Canning and Storage of Food Stuffs
Vegetable Gardening
Poultry Raising
Russia—Our Ally Republic
Social Service in Wartime
Foreign Trade Expansion
War Poems
Tales from the Trenches
Uncle Sam's Navy
Keeping Fit in Wartime
Why We Are at War
Courage

The success of the "one million books for one million soldiers" program is noted on both the personal level and the national level. Jennie Gilbert Jerome was first exposed to working with the New Haven Public Library during the war years when she collected books for soldiers—just as her brother had asked from the western front. She became a branch librarian at Dixwell and later served as the art librarian at the main branch between 1922 and 1952. She amassed an art clipping collection that was said to rival the one held by the *New York Times*. The success of the book and library programs of World War I meant that during World War II, the federal government created a centralized book program to ship more than 122 million small, lightweight paperbacks to soldiers overseas. Like the fighting on the western front itself—half mired in the previous century and half looking ahead—the library programs of World War I were mired in the ways of the past but, looking forward, dedicated to the importance of books and the librarians who care for them. Much like today's multifaceted fast-paced world, librarians were—and are—expected to be familiar with the broadest range of lines of inquiry and the latest technologies and methods for finding and disseminating information. Although the last vestiges of the card catalogue, bookplate and stamped and dated card glued to the inside cover are just about gone from twenty-first-century society, today's librarians continue to serve city residents and soldiers just as the World War I generation did.

Jennie Gilbert Jerome working with students at the card catalogue, New Haven Free Public Library, 1940. Jerome, seen at the right, wore her hair in a dated "coronet" style, from her school days, and preferred to dress in black. The hardworking New Haven students wear bobby socks and saddle shoes. Times changed, but Jerome's life remained dated to the time of her brother's death—she never married and lived in the family home at 987 Forest Street until her death in 1979. *Courtesy of the Local History Room, New Haven Free Public Library.*

6

SAINTS AND SOLDIERS

The Red Cross, YMCA/YWCA and Knights of Columbus

It is a long, long way to the old Green.

—Reverend Oscar E. Maurer, pastor of Center Church on the western front with the YMCA, July 21, 1918

At its core, the city of New Haven, Connecticut, is a place profoundly shaped by its religious heritage. Founded as the Colony of New Haven in 1638 by little more than five hundred immigrants from England, the Puritans formulated a church and state legal system with strict codes of social conduct. This chapter is concerned with the programs staffed on the homefront by groups with religious connections and with the religious leaders who left the city to serve on the western front during World War I. New Haven's Christian community was greatly expanded in the nineteenth century, due to the influx of new immigrants, such as the Irish and Italians. During the war, leaders from the city's oldest congregational parishes, including the First Church of Christ—the church that had existed from the colony's very beginning, located in the center of the center square (thus, its informal name: Center Church)—were joined by Roman Catholics and people from many other faiths, including Orthodox Christians and Jews, all of whom contributed to the war effort. The Joint Jewish Relief Committee, for example, solicited $75,000 from city residents "for the benefit of the Jewish war sufferers and for the welfare work for Jewish Soldiers and Sailors" as part of the "closer welding of all creeds" spearheaded by the Knights of

Knights of Columbus, William Balfour Ker, lithograph, 1917. Pictured here is a young priest holding a crucifix in his right hand (the good hand) toward heaven. Infantrymen and navy sailors kneel around him, with bayonets pointed upward, reminiscent of the crown of thorns worn by Jesus during his crucifixion. In the distance, American flags, flags of the Allies and flames burn around vessels. The red cheeks and eyelashes of the priest reinforce youth—before all the men pictured are changed by their war experiences. Balfour Ker, whose family emigrated from Scotland, trained with illustrator Howard Pyle. *Library of Congress.*

Columbus in February 1918. While most Americans are familiar with the enormous social contributions the Red Cross, the YMCA and the Knights of Columbus have given—and continued to give—on both the domestic and international stage, very little is remembered of the individuals who left their comfortable posts to become "soldiers" on the western front. Clarence Edwards, commander of the Yankee Division and later a major general of the U.S. Army, called the serving religious community "part of the soul of that division." This chapter is a brief glimpse into some of the service these New Haven men and women from religious and humanitarian organizations provided during World War I.

RED CROSS

Famously founded by Clara Barton and her colleagues in Washington, D.C., in 1881, the American Red Cross addressed the continuing needs of veterans suffering the devastating effects of the Civil War. Under Barton's leadership, the organization established itself with local chapters around the country focusing on first aid, water safety, nursing and public health. But less than two decades after Barton's retirement, World War I created tremendous growth for the organization, which grew from just over one hundred local chapters to almost four thousand by 1918. These chapters were served by more than twenty million adults and eleven million Junior Red Cross members. During the war years, the Red Cross raised funds for programs that supported soldiers and injured veterans on the homefront, staffed hospitals and drove ambulances on the western front and dealt directly with the Spanish flu outbreak on both fronts in 1918. In the Elm City, the New Haven Chapter of the American Red Cross ran canning kitchens and programs for women, young and old alike, as well as led campaigns to knit sweaters for "soldiers in the frost-bound trenches." The Red Cross also directed other groups, such as the Girls Patriotic League of New Haven, in making ten thousand surgical gauze dressings and provided lunches, smokes and "other comforts" to the soldiers going to the front. At one point, the New Haven Chapter of the American Red Cross claimed that one-fifth of the city's population was a member.

It is hard to find an American soldier not aware of, and grateful to, the American Red Cross for its efforts—especially for those on the western front. In World War II, New Haven Monuments Man Deane Keller mentions the organization in a letter home from Italy, writing, "I cannot say enough about this organization. Every one of their establishments has been first class and they do a bang up job." In World War I, New Haven aviator Gilbert Nelson Jerome also described the work of the Red Cross in a letter home to his family:

> *The Red Cross continues to be most popular. I eat all of my meals there. This noon we had asparagus, chicken, spinach, rice, pudding, bread and tea. The American women who work here lend a home atmosphere that is very fine. They have to work pretty hard feeding that big crowd of hungry men three times a day, and I guess they get tired before the day is through. It is a sort of thankless task, something like running church suppers continuously, but most of them are young enough to stand the grind very well.*

But the Red Cross did hard work, too, in another realm: that of acting as a liaison for American families, providing information regarding wounding or death. A case in point was the Jerome family of New Haven. It was through the Red Cross that Elizabeth and Jennie, discussed in chapter 1, first learned that Gilbert was missing in action. And it was also through the Red Cross that the women learned he was killed in action. As Elizabeth wrote in her memoir about her son's life and death, "[T]he Red Cross did everything in their power to obtain information for me through Berne, Switzerland, who received word from the German Red Cross that he was buried in the German Military Cemetery, near Blâmont with full military honors."

The Red Cross also contributed significantly to another area of relief work: that of rebuilding countries destroyed by more than four years of war. New Havener Thomas C. Farnham, commissioned a lieutenant colonel with the American Red Cross, traveled to Serbia to oversee rebuilding efforts in the "wreckage of war." Railroad facilities had to be rebuilt, electricity only ran for a few hours every day and diseases such as typhus broke out. Farnham established headquarters in two areas of the country, at Saloniki and Belgrade, from where he could oversee operations to help Serbians rebuild—and provide instructions in "healthy living." Cleanliness was clearly a part of the American Red Cross ethos; as one newspaper reported, "[T]he relief force supervises and cleans and cleans and cleans and supervises and then cleans."

Another New Havener, the Reverend Robert C. Denison of United Church on the Green, was commissioned a major in the American Red Cross and sent to Albania. There Denison organized one hundred workers

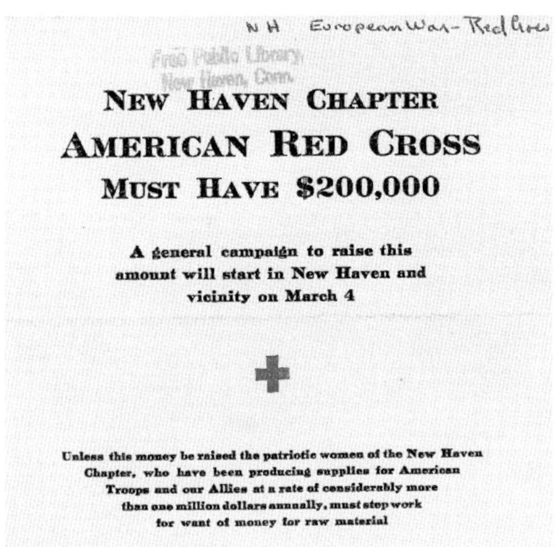

NEW HAVEN CHAPTER
AMERICAN RED CROSS
MUST HAVE $200,000

A general campaign to raise this amount will start in New Haven and vicinity on March 4

Unless this money be raised the patriotic women of the New Haven Chapter, who have been producing supplies for American Troops and our Allies at a rate of considerably more than one million dollars annually, must stop work for want of money for raw material

"New Haven Chapter of the American Red Cross Must Have $200,000" campaign card. During the course of 1917-1918, the American Red Cross raised $400 million dollars used for "raw materials" and other programmatic and administrative costs associated to their extensive work on the home front and the western front. The Red Cross targeted "the mothers and the children of the New Haven men at the front" to make sure they were cared for. Administrators boasted, "the production record of the New Haven Chapter of the American Red Cross was double that of other cities." *Courtesy of the Local History Room, New Haven Free Public Library.*

who needed to enter Albania on pack mules and oxcarts through narrow mountain passes, since railroad lines were destroyed. Denison helped to establish relief centers and provide medical supervision. According to Denison's report to the Red Cross, parts of which were published in the *Journal-Courier*, "[T]he poor of the city who were to receive goods were summoned by the mayor in the ancient way, by sending out through the city a crier who beats a drum at different corners." Albanians apparently had enough food, but their "lack of clothing was apparent and pitiful." Children had almost no clothing and stood shivering in the street, and many women had no shoes. At the time, poor people—peasants—made all of their own clothing from sheep's wool, which had been almost impossible to access to during the war years. Denison oversaw the delivery of both food and clothing from the United States, including sacks of rice and sugar, shawls, sweaters and even "one huge box of corduroy clothing." Although the distribution of goods was celebrated, there was not enough. One hundred shawls were given out, but one thousand "shivering and undernourished" women needed them.

Farnham's and Denison's reports of their time in Macedonia alternated between "desolation and thanksgiving." It wasn't easy on the Red Cross relief workers to see the amount of need. After distributing their meager goods, it was apparent how desperate people were, one result of war that is often forgotten in histories that focus on regiments, battles and military strategy. Children were starved to death, families were torn apart and possessions and houses were destroyed. Denison described meeting Serbians, whom he praised as a "quiet and modest" people, who were "determined and

"You can help," American Red Cross poster, Władysław Teodor "W.T." Benda, 1918. Born in Poland, Benda moved to the United States at the turn of the twentieth century, becoming a naturalized citizen in 1911. He studied at the Art Students League in New York and was a member of the Society of Illustrators and National Society of Mural Painters. He designed posters for both Poland and the United States, most focusing on relief efforts, during World War I and II. The *Journal Courier* reported that the "army of Red Cross workers in New Haven" knitted 2,632 sweaters for soldiers on the front. *Library of Congress.*

[showed] enduring heroism." He saw Serbians returning to their country from Bulgaria wearing nothing but sacks of cloth tied around their waists and called it a "privilege to try and help them," but "it [the war] all seems very horrible and useless."

YMCA/YWCA

Like the Red Cross, which first began life as a European organization in Switzerland, the Young Men's Christian Association (YMCA) first appeared in London in 1844. Its focus on helping the downtrodden in a quickly industrializing world appealed to missionaries and Christian social activists, and the first American chapter was established in Boston by 1851. YMCAs were built across the United States, serving people across gender, race and ethnic lines, thus making their efforts for soldiers in World War I easily transferable to both the homefront and western front. By the end of the war, the Y had established 1,500 "canteens" in the United States and France and also ran another 4,000 "huts" for religious use and recreation for soldiers. On the homefront, the YMCA's female counterpart, the YWCA, ran training programs for women from its building at 568 Chapel Street. These organizations, like the Red Cross, also raised funds, resulting in $235 million (or $4.3 billion in today's currency). In a newspaper article about Camp Devens in Ayers, Massachusetts, where many "New Haven Draft Men" were sent for training, the impact of the Y was described by one journalist in the October 7, 1917 issue of the *New Haven Register*:

> *Here is where the YMCA plays it part and the work of this body is little short of wonderful. Besides the main building, the YMCA has had erected a building for each organization with a moving picture auditorium, where movies are given free, writing desks with paper and envelopes gratis at the disposition of soldiers; a Victoria with many records and innumerable games. Until the main library of the cantonment is built, the YMCA is running a small library in each building where the men can obtain both good fiction and instructional books. Three Knights of Columbus buildings are nearly completed and this will add other havens for an evening of pleasure with its games, books, pool table, etc.*

One New Havener, the Reverend J.W. Laird, a director of religious activities with the YMCA in New Haven, became well known at Camp Meade in Maryland. Described as "robust in his Christianity and energetic in his leadership," Laird went "among the men like a real shepherd and a militant dominie [minister] such as an army camp should demand." Laird helped soldiers become Bible study leaders in each of their barracks but was also known as the "best raconteur" in the camp.

In 1918, the letters of another New Havener, the Reverend Oscar E. Maurer, were printed in Elm City newspapers. Maurer had a one-year leave of absence from Center Church and worked under the auspices of the YMCA, supervising the erection and daily workings of huts along the front. Facilitating the rebuilding efforts from a series of huts, Maurer struggled to keep relations friendly between the French, the armies and the Y staff. The shape of his work was described in the following letter, dated April 2, 1918:

> *The little Ford fairly groaned when I cranked her up, but we have accomplished a lot of work. I have established two new locations…have hunted up a couple of huts away from everywhere which needed magazines and paper; settled a dispute among the staff of another hut, preached twice and ran out of gasoline in the midst of a railway shipyard, where I was trying to find some of our supplies that were too slow in coming.*

Maurer even baptized three American soldiers who were leaving the next day for the front. He, too, traveled back and forth from the front, as soldiers did, administering and assisting wherever needed. He described his time at the front in another letter dated June 1, 1918: "Yesterday was our first Memorial Day in France. In the morning I held service in a tiny God's-acre on the line. Never, never have I heard a silence like the silence of a lull. All the world might be dead."

Knights of Columbus

Although the youngest of the religious/humanitarian organizations to work for soldiers both on the homefront and the western front, the Knights of Columbus was fully homegrown. Founded in the basement of St. Mary's Church in New Haven in 1881 by a young Irish American priest named Father Michael McGivney, the organization grew into the

"Everybody Welcome! Everything Free!" Sheet music, with words by Thomas Kelly and music by Frederick A. Durbin, 1918. Illustrated with an image of a K of C hut, simple wooden structures built in cantonments on the homefront and in France on the western front, a soldier is shown making his way into the warm glow, where inside a Casey waits, ready to provide basic amenities that helped soldiers deal with life away from home. *Library of Congress.*

world's largest Catholic fraternal organization, assisted in no small part by World War I. That the Knights of Columbus followed American soldiers into war isn't surprising—many of McGivney's first committee members had been soldiers in the Ninth Regiment Connecticut Volunteers (the state's Irish American regiment) during the Civil War. Knights of Columbus members thus considered themselves knights going into battle for their country and their faith. And in fact, Connecticut's only state-sponsored Civil War monument with a Latin cross engraved on its shaft is located in New Haven, demonstrating the city's long involvement with religion, faith and war.

Like the YMCA, the Knights of Columbus via their Committee on War Activities ran huts on the western front that became famous due to the phrase "Everybody Welcome, Everything Free." The huts were staffed by a secretary (called "Caseys" by the Americans for "K of C") and a chaplain and provided free books, stationery—1,800 tons of stationery and envelopes were purchased for soldiers to use—candy (gumdrops, hard candy and chocolate), cigarettes, chewing gum and entertainment and sports equipment, as well as Catholic religious services.

Appreciation for the YMCA and K of C huts derived from the safe, warm, friendly spaces each hut provided, reinforced in the image portrayed on the sheet music here: "Gee! I'm broke and I want a smoke / The world looks blue to me / Ready to die of hunger / But here we are at a K.C. hut / Where everybody's welcome, and everything is free." After the war, educational programs were sponsored by the Knights for returning soldiers. In addition, much like Elizabeth Jerome and her daughter, Jennie, the K of C sponsored a pilgrimage to Metz, France, in 1920, where a new statue of

Handkerchief, khaki/cotton embroidered in white with "K of C." A Knights of Columbus Casey (secretary) might have worn this handkerchief while "serving the boys" on the homefront and the western front. *Courtesy of the West Haven Veterans Museum & Learning Center.*

Lafayette, Paul Wayland Bartlett, bronze equestrian, 1920, Metz, France (destroyed). Bartlett, born in New Haven, lived in Paris for the duration of his short life, the primary urban center for the study of sculpture, a tradition dating to Rodin. Bartlett first created *Lafayette on Horseback* for the Louvre, donated to France from the United States on July 4, 1908. This copy in Metz, donated by the Knights of Columbus, was destroyed by the German occupation forces in World War II. A third copy was installed in Hartford, Connecticut, on Armistice Day in 1932, seven years after the sculptor's death. *Author's collection.*

the Marquis de Lafayette was dedicated to the city from which Lafayette left for the United States in 1777 and where American troops landed in 1917 to enter the western front.

In addition to the three organizations discussed, several of New Haven's religious leaders went to war attached to the 102nd Regiment, Yankee Division. The Reverend Orville A. Petty was a senior chaplain of the 102nd; one of the projects he led from the western front was a fundraiser for the regimental band. 4,467.78 francs were raised and sent from New Haven to France. Petty was clergy in the Plymouth Congregational Church—the same church where the Jerome family worshipped—and occasionally he and Gilbert exchanged letters. He, Dr. Oscar Maurer of Center Church and the Reverend Roy Martin Houghton of the Church of the Redeemer attended burials in "No Man's Land," especially watching out for the bodies of their regiment from New Haven who had "gone over the top." Letters from the local pastors often appeared in the city's newspapers, including news that Petty had earned a *Croix de Guerre* and a Belgian award for his service. Representative John Q. Tilson of New Haven, a member of a wartime congressional committee, traveled to France in 1918. In the *Register* (Tilson spoke with the paper briefly before traveling to Washington, D.C., to deliver his report), Tilson said, "[F]rom the time we reached France, clear through until we came to Coblenz, wherever we went there was some New Haven man doing his share in this important work of the American army." Tilson was able to pin a decoration from the king of Belgium onto Chaplain Petty's breast. Glenna Bigelow, who lived on Howe Street and was nursing in a hospital on the front, wrote home:

> *By the way—who do you think came into my ward the other day? None other than Dr. Petty himself—his regiment is not many miles from here, and several of his boys are in my ward, whom he came to see. You can imagine how wonderful it was to see somebody from home! I quizzed the boys after he went, and it appears that they are just wild about him—"The Fighting Parson" as they call him, they could not say enough about him, and just yesterday he was decorated by Major General Edwards and a French general with the "Croix de Guerre" for bravery and devotion in action....* [I]*t seems that he goes right over the top with the men....New Haven should be very proud of her Hero Chaplain!*

The Reverned R.M. Houghton from Church of the Redeemer also served with the 102nd on the western front, appearing at Château-Thierry when the

26th division relieved the Marines. When he was back in the United States, his church held a welcome home ceremony, where Hougton told stories from the front that were then reported in the city's newspapers. One story Houghton related from his experiences with the 102nd Infantry at Château-Thierry was the moment when the regiment was unexpectedly delayed two hours; Houghton described the men as "much depressed, because they wished to 'get at the enemy at once.'" Houghton said of the 102nd, "Nothing in the world could have stopped them," when they were called to go over the top. Houghton was also with the 102nd when several members were captured by the *Boche*, or German soldiers. Some of the experiences of the 102nd are discussed in the next chapter.

7

SUMMER 1918, *BOCHE*, BOMBS AND BAYONETS

The 102nd Regiment "Yankee Division" Over There

When aviator Gilbert Nelson Jerome went to France in September 1917, he described his excitement in a letter to his mother in New Haven, "I cannot get over the feeling that we are off on a sort of grand pleasure tour, in which Uncle Sam pays the bills and conducts the tour." As seen, his experiences were unique to aviators—and thus much different from the New Haveners who enlisted or were drafted as infantry (sometimes called "Sammies" by the French for Uncle Sam) or as gunners and all manner of support staff from medics and cooks to farriers and ambulance drivers. The forward line, the infantry experience, consisted of constant rotation—movement back and forth from the trenches—holding the line, inching the line forward and getting pushed back, all the while surrounded by destroyed villages and farmland, acres of barbed and trip wire, gas attacks, flame throwers and a "volley of thunderbolts" at all hours of the night and day, which one doughboy described as a "living hell of fire and death." While Jerome described his admiration for the men and machines of the air, another New Havener, infantryman Philip English, remembered in his scrapbook that "one could not imagine that machines of man [on land] could create such horrible and wide-spread devastation."

The American Expeditionary Force entered France from the shore of Point de Grave—the same place from which the Marquis de Lafayette left France in 1777 to assist the American Revolution. This was especially pertinent to the doughboys of the Yankee Division (YD), who saw themselves as direct descendants of the militiamen—the underdogs fighting the

COLONEL JOHN HENRY PARKER
UNITED STATES ARMY
IN TRIBUTE TO A COURAGEOUS FIGHTER AND GENTLEMAN,
COL. JOHN HENRY "MACHINE GUN" PARKER, WHO COMMANDED THE
102nd U.S. INFANTRY OF THE 26th (YANKEE) DIVISION IN THE
GREAT WORLD WAR, THIS TABLET IS ERECTED BY NEW HAVEN
CHAPTER YANKEE DIVISION VETERANS ASSOCIATION IN
COOPERATION WITH THE FEDERAL ART PROJECT OF THE

British—in Lexington and Concord. Members of the 102nd Field Artillery painted a Revolutionary War–era cannon on their metal helmets, a reference yet again to their history, while the 102nd Infantry painted the Charter Oak. At some point, even Sergeant Stubby became a painted marking, as seen in one historic photograph of a unit of doughboys, all shouldering gas mask bags with a stenciled image of the dog. Other units within the YD using Revolutionary-era markings included the 26th Division Headquarters Troops, which had the figure of Paul Revere riding a horse with the date "1775," and the 101st Engineer Train, which had the Bunker Hill Monument and "1776," painted on their respective helmets.

Although units, regiments and divisions identified themselves separately, as indicated by Pershing's statement opening this chapter, American troops fought together as a single army on the western front—all except for the two African American divisions mentioned in chapter 2. According to the Imperial War Museum, the "American Expeditionary Force became an integral part of the Allied strategy of 'rolling offensives' over the period of August to November 1918." This strategy, which historians now call the "Hundred Days," was a well-coordinated effort across the Allied armies resulting in the defeat of the Central powers. In this work, regiments of the Yankee Division would play their part; the division, in fact, "spent just ten days in a rest area." The rest of the time, the Yankee Division—with Sergeant Stubby in tow—was in rotation at the front.

The first American regiments began shipping out to Europe in the summer of 1917, but things sped up in the fall of that year and continued into the spring of 1918, when ten thousand American troops were arriving in Europe every day. The first American unit organized as a division in the United States and transported complete to France, the 101st Regiment of the Yankee Division, reached Saint Nazaire on September 21, 1917, with other regiments, including the 102nd. In the trenches, the soldiers of the 26th

Opposite: *Colonel John Henry Parker*, Michele Martino, bas-relief plaque, painted plaster, 1939. "In tribute to a courageous fighter and gentleman, Col. John Henry 'Machine Gun' Parker, who commanded the 102nd U.S. Infantry of the 26th (Yankee) Division in the Great World War, this tablet is erected by New Haven Chapter Yankee Division Veterans Association in Cooperation with the Federal Art Project of the Works Progress Administration. MCDXXXIX." (The Roman numerals should read MCMXXXIX, for 1939, not 1439). Martino completed a second plaque to General James A. Haggerty the following year, 1940. Both were hung in the Goffe Street Armory until the building was closed in 2009. Earlier, Martino designed the Spanish-American Memorial, *The Hiker*, in Edgewood Park (1924) and the bas-relief figures on the World War I Memorial Flagpole on the green (1929). *Courtesy of the West Haven Veterans Museum & Learning Center.*

Lafayette, we are here!

—Lieutenant Colonel Charles E. Stanton, Yale and AEF, address at the tomb of Lafayette, Paris, July 4, 1917

were assigned to the 162nd Infantry, 11th French Army Corps, which General Clarence Edwards called the "godfather" of the YD. Journalist Frank Palmer Sibley—who coined the moniker "Yankee Division" during a press conference in 1917—wrote, "[W]e were clearly understood to be amateurs in the war," but the YD would learn and earn respect quickly. They engaged in the first two battles in which Americans fought without support of the French infantry, entering the line in the Chemin des Dames ("the Ladies Path") on February 6, 1918. The division endured two days of intense bombardment with gas attacks in March. Then, in April, Company E of the 102nd fought in the Toul sector in the Ardennes, where battle lines had not shifted since 1914. This would lead to the Battle of Seicheprey on April 20—where "New Haven lads received [their] baptism of fire," the most important memory marker for New Haven in the postwar years. Although the New Englanders were not successful on their own and suffered great casualties—French infantry came to back them up, thus engendering criticism that the division was not ready for action at the front—the *Boche*, who had had the high ground in addition to 3,600 infantry and two hundred cannons, noted that the Yankees had put up "stubborn resistance which neither the French nor English would be able to put up any longer."

Seicheprey, a small village of three hundred, had stood on the front line for four years of war. Seventeen New Haveners died at Seicheprey, most of them machine gunners from Company D and E. In one instance, the Boche poured a stream of liquid fire into a pill box of the 102nd—"screams and groans of agony" were heard. Soldiers fought hand to hand here, using cleavers and knives, chunks of wood and stone, whatever men could get their hands on. For their efforts, Colonel Parker and the 102nd Infantry were cited in a general order of the French 32nd Army Corps on April 26, 1918—only six days after the bloodiest loss in the Elm City's war history to that point. Then, on April 28, 1918, in a field near Boucq, the 102nd's regimental flag was decorated with the *Croix de Guerre* by French general Fenelon F.G. Passaga. "I am proud to decorate the flag of a regiment which has shown such fortitude and courage," he said. "I am proud to decorate the flag of a nation which has come to aid in the fight for liberty." Thus, the 102nd Regiment of the YD became the very first American unit to be honored by a foreign country for

Right: Doughboy wool service coat called a "blouse," with 102nd Field Artillery Regiment helmet, gas mask bag and service medal. *Courtesy of the West Haven Veterans Museum & Learning Center.*

Below: Yankee Division moving into the Toul sector, 1918. Curious French children watch the YD march with their ammunition train into Soulosse in northeastern France, late March 1918. The area around Toul, a medieval town on the Moselle River, later in the year became the site from which the Allied armies launched two large operations: the St. Mihiel Offensive and the Meuse-Argonne Offensive, both in September 1918. The YD took part in both offensives; New Haveners such as Corporal Timothy Ahearn and Sergeant Stubby participated in both with the 102nd Regiment. *Courtesy of the Whitney Library, New Haven Museum.*

Marne advance, July 18, 1918. Wire obstacles, seen in the foreground, were laid out in simple fence lines to elaborate patterns, meant to slow down attackers on the offense. Trip wire was planted in the ground attached to stakes, which channeled incoming attackers into areas where machine guns were positioned, thus resulting in high casualty rates during World War I. The pattern seen here is called the "double apron" fence, purposely designed in a horizontal and vertical pattern spread across open land. *Courtesy of the Whitney Library, New Haven Museum.*

exceptional bravery in combat. In addition, 117 members of the regiment received the award, including its commander, Colonel George H. Shelton. The State of Connecticut remembered the loss of life at Seicheprey in 1925 by installing a memorial fountain in the village.

The offensives of the Aisne-Marne and the Champagne-Marne occurred in June 1918. All units of the YD fought at the Aisne-Marne July 18–25, and with August came the gigantic Allied push against the enemy strongholds of Château-Thierry. General Degouette of the Sixth Army said of the YD: "The 26th alone is responsible for the whole Allied advance on the Marne. They are shock troops, par excellence!" All units again participated in the St. Mihiel Offensive September 12–13. The 102nd Infantry went on to participate in the Meuse-Argonne Offensive on September 26, earning the unit the *Croix de Guerre* for "meritorious conduct." Finally, all units of the

YD served in the last offensive of the war, November 7–11, 1918, under which the objective was to "secure possession of the heights of the Meuse, and to follow up German retirement in the direction of Azannes and Les Jumelles D'Orne." The YD served in the trenches an aggregate of seven months, or 210 days. Of the YD, casualties in battle were 421 officers and 11,534 enlisted men for a total of 11,955 deaths. More than 3,000 men were gassed, and the bodies of 283 were never recovered. A captured confidential document of the 19th German Army supports the argument that though the YD went in to World War I with little experience: "The Twenty-sixth American Division is a fighting division which has proven its qualities in battles on various parts of the front."

Addressing the morale of soldiers at the front was of paramount importance for military leaders, but the relationship was reciprocal—morale also needed vigilance on the homefront. One newspaper stated, "[Y]ou must tell the soldier, the American soldier, that he is fighting for his home or he won't fight." At the same time, mothers of dead soldiers needed to know that their sacrifice was not in vain. Although there was a great deal of patriotic and sentimental public statements and speeches, the reality of the fight was one of total destruction. One New Havener who died in the midst of the Hundred Days, Lieutenant Harold Ludington Hemingway (1893–1918), was buried in France after being wounded on October 21, 1918. Hemingway lived with his parents, Mr. and Mr. James Hemingway, at 325 Temple Street, attended Center Church and graduated from Yale in 1914. As noted earlier, Dr. Maurer, the pastor of Center Church, was in France at the time, helping to bury men found in no man's land—a stretch of open land between opposing armies. Although attached to the YMCA, Maurer found the 102nd Infantry and presided over the burial of many soldiers, including those from New Haven, no matter their regiment, including Hemingway, who fought with the 104th. Only 15 percent of the Yankee Division returned home alive in 1919. Many others lived with physical and mental ailments for the rest of their lives. Death was not always a result of battle wounds—more than twenty-five New Haveners died from disease, in addition to accidental deaths both in camps on the homefront and on the western front.

We came American. We shall remain American and go into battle with Old Glory over our heads. I will not parcel out American boys.

—General John J. "Black Jack" Pershing, commander, AEF, 1918

Connecticut Memorial at Seicheprey, France, 1923. The memorial consists of a stone fountain with a bronze tablet inserted into the façade. Water is released from a man's bearded face into the basin below. "To the Commune of Seicheprey/To Commemorate the Service of the 102nd Infantry, 26th Division/A Regiment of the American Army Recruited from Citizens of Connecticut's Defenders of Seicheprey April 20, 1918/In the firm belief that friendship of Frenchmen and Americans sealed in this place in battle shall serve the cause of peace among all nations/This memorial is presented by the Men and Women of Connecticut, 1923." *Courtesy of the Whitney Library, New Haven Museum.*

As noted in chapter 2, soldiers on the front had to contend not only with the Spanish flu but also with "trench fever," an equally insidious bacterial disease carried by lice and spread by vermin—those creatures that lived in the trenches alongside humans. Although trench fever did not kill outright like the Spanish flu, soldiers became debilitated, with large numbers of men across the AEF and Allies out of commission due to their weakened states. Six noncombatant soldiers from the 102nd Regiment and sixty others volunteered to take trench fever bacteria in a hospital on the front, in a study to try and find how the disease was transmitted. The men, such as Sergeant Raymond Kenney who lived on Elm Street with his aunt and uncle, were described as "dangerously ill for several months" after receiving the bacteria. Each man lost between twenty and twenty-five pounds and could only lie in his hospital bed—one newspaper described men so weak that even when bombing was close (the hospital was behind British front lines), they were too weak to get under their beds for cover. The fever affected the eyes of its victims, so reading was impossible. Many of the men suffered relapses, but all survived the experiment, "anxious to get back to their units." In addition to Sergeant Kenney, Arthur R. Fahy, William T. Daley, Ralph A. Walker, William H. Reed and William J. Slater, all New Haveners were part of this "trying ordeal."

These New Haven men/guinea pigs were noncombatant soldiers who stepped up to the plate because they knew their fellow Elm City brothers were at the front. This included two friends from Fair Haven, the Irish American enclave of the city: Timothy Francis "Timmy" Ahearn and John

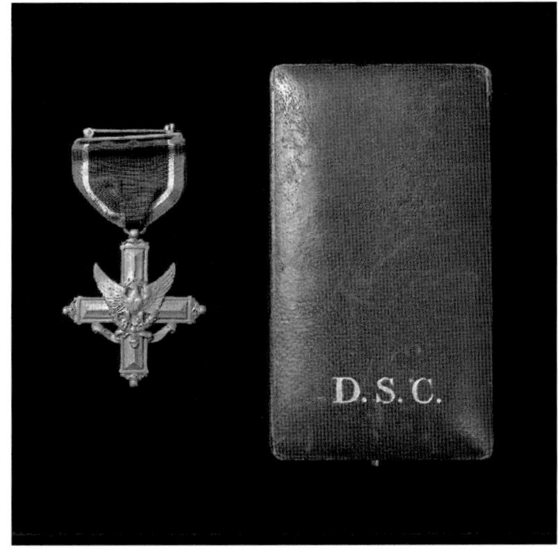

Distinguished Service Cross belonging to John Thomas "Jack" Dillon, 1918. The cross is the second-highest honor awarded in the U.S. Army, behind the Medal of Honor. Soldiers such as Jack Dillon and Timothy Ahearn were awarded the DSC for "extreme gallantry and risk of life." The medal consists of a bronze cross with four equal arms hanging from a red, white, and blue ribbon. A spread-winged eagle sits at the center, and a scroll below bearing the inscription "For Valor" appears as support under the arms of the cross. A laurel wreath of victory encircles the eagle. *Courtesy of John T. Dillon, Esq.*

The Infantry, the Infantry,
With dirt behind their ears,
You cannot beat the Infantry,
In a hundred thousand years.

—typed inscription in Philip H. English's World War I diary, 102nd Regiment, 1917–19

Thomas "Jack" Dillon. Both were members of Company C of the 102nd Regiment, which had been decimated at Seicheprey, and both men later received the Distinguished Service Cross—Ahearn for actions at Verdun and Dillon for carrying messages in no man's land at Château-Thierry. Ahearn was the only soldier from New Haven known to have served in every battle in France, and although his story is more well known than Dillon's (and is discussed in the next chapter), their intertwined lives before and during war demonstrate the close-knit communities of American "brothers" who often fought together on the western front.

Dillon was born in Ennis, County Clare, Ireland, in 1895. His father immigrated to the United States, with Dillon's mother, elder brother and himself following the next year. The family lived at 56 Bright Street in New Haven, and the Dillon boys attended St. Francis School. After graduating, Dillon went to work as a clerk for the Knights of Columbus on Chapel Street, while his brother, Patrick, was employed at the Marlin Firearms Company (where Ahearn also worked). Dillon, like many young men from his neighborhood, wrestled with the Maple Athletic Club, played football and basketball and was also a notable tennis player—playing on New Haven's semipro teams. Club members also raced canoes and boats on the Quinnipiac River. In New Haven, they had often played on rival teams, but when the United States entered World War I, young Catholics enlisted together in the "old Sarsfield Guard," which became Company C of the 102nd Regiment. In France, Dillon fought at Seicheprey, Vaux and Château-Thierry. He was at Château-Thierry during the July 20–22, 1918 offensive, where he was wounded. The Knights of Columbus clerk refused to go to the rear but volunteered to act as a runner, carrying messages through enemy barrage. Later, on the same day, he voluntarily joined a platoon and fought with it in a successful attack against enemy lines.

The athleticism of Americans at the time, developed from the friendly rivalries of neighborhood clubs like the Maple—and epitomized in New Haven, perhaps, by the famous Yale/Harvard football games at the Yale Bowl and by Walter Camp's exercise program—made an impression on German forces in France. One document describes the Germans as noticing

Maple Athletic Club, New Haven, 1916. Six of the young men seen in this photograph would become members of Company C of the 102nd Regiment, 26th Division, including (*top row*) Jim Quinn (*second from left*), Harold Shields (*third from left*), Timothy Ahearn (*fourth from left*), Jim Coleman (*fifth from right*) and Jack Dillon (*fourth from right*). In the front row, Ed Stockpole (*second from left*) also served in Company C. *Courtesy of John T. Dillon, Esq.*

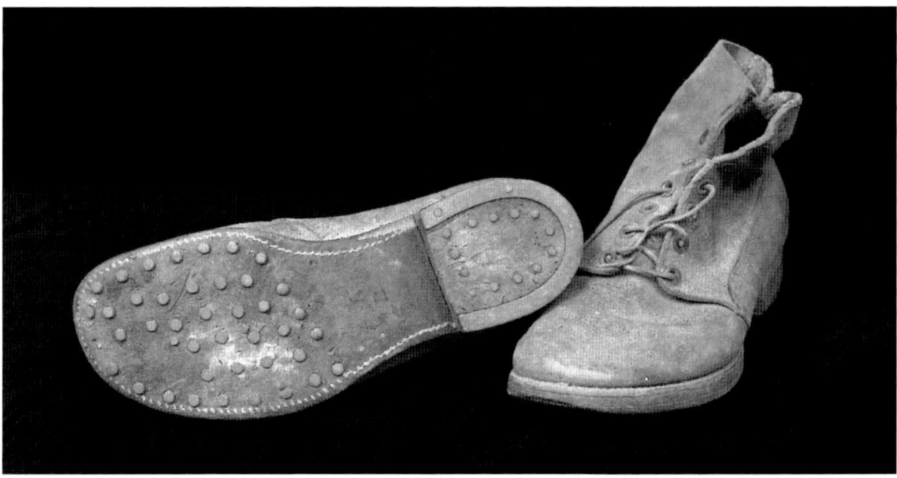

Jack Dillon's trench boots, circa 1917–19. Dillon's standard-issue leather boots are typical of those worn by doughboys in American, British and French armies. Worn-down hobnails can still be seen on the bottom, as well as the horseshoe-like iron heel, both of which were intended to help soldiers navigate cold mud. The boots were made of tanned cowhide but were not waterproof, leading to a common problem for infantry: trench foot. Later, the trench boot was redesigned for better waterproofing, renamed the "Pershing Boot." *Courtesy of John T. Dillon, Esq.*

how athletic the doughboys were, labeling them as "strong, healthy men [with] beardless faces." The Maple Athletic Club became the scene of many farewell parties for men who left the city to serve overseas, and after the war, veteran Maples and their wives continued to meet regularly. The club put on vaudeville-like performances for fun and to raise money—the centerpiece of the show a male chorus, with female dancers. The "Maple Show" was so popular, Poli's Theater on Church Street booked the show for their venue (Poli's likewise booked Sergeant Stubby, "New Haven's Own 102nd Mascot," for three nights in May 1919). YD veterans and Maple Athletic Club members like Jack Dillon continued to remember Seicheprey Day in New Haven until the 1970s, raising funds for the erection of a monument to their friend Timothy Ahearn. While many YD veterans in New Haven went on to live robust and satisfying lives, others were not so fortunate. Jack Dillon became a U.S. citizen in 1919, married Marie Reilly in 1930, had three children and went to work in his family's business. The story of his Maple Athletic Club mate and Company C brother Timothy Ahearn—whose smiling face looks to the camera in 1916 from the banks of the Quinnipiac River—turned out differently.

8

CITY MEMORY IN BRONZE

New Haven World War I Monuments

The City of New Haven began erecting markers referencing war as early as the eighteenth century—there exists a grave marker in Grove Street Cemetery noting one man's death in the Invasion of New Haven in 1779. As seen, the City of New Haven was deeply involved with the events of World War I, and this, in combination with active veterans' groups during the 1920s and 1930s, created the momentum for major new monuments and memorials to be added to the landscape of the city. This chapter looks at public monument-making for World War I in the Elm City, coalescing in three important additions to the public art and memorial landscape: the World War I Memorial Flagpole and Honor Roll on the green, the Timothy Ahearn Memorial in West River Memorial Park and the 102nd Regiment Marker on Derby Avenue near the Yale Bowl. These three "community gestures" are in addition to the memorializing done on the campus of Yale University.

Yale University began its memory making in bronze and granite in 1926–27 with the installation of the Yale Alumni War Memorial on Hewitt Quadrangle (discussed in the next chapter); the City of New Haven followed closely behind, erecting its first World War I memorial in 1929. The site chosen was none other than the very heart of the city: the center of the lower green, which, as described in chapter 2, was intrinsically important to city identity. The New Haven Green was then—and remains to this day—owned and managed by a private group of citizens formally called the Committee of the Proprietors of Common and Undivided Lands at New

Corporal Timothy Ahearn Memorial, Karl Frederick Lang (artist), Maxwell & Pagano (installers), bronze, dedicated November 11, 1937. The monument was commissioned by members of the Maple Athletic Club and the New Haven Chapter of the Yankee Division Veterans Association. Fortuitously, the Federal Art Project of the Works Progress Administration offered an opportunity for community groups to partner with the government in creating works of art for the public. The cost was shared. This is the only bronze monument created under the WPA program in New Haven and served as the site for annual Seicheprey Day observances. *Courtesy of the Connecticut State Library.*

Haven, a group of five self-electing private citizens who manage the green space on behalf of the city and its residents. Not surprisingly, as the center of the city, the green has been identified as a place for erecting public art, monuments and memorials over the course of more than two centuries, but very few proposals have made it to the construction phase, due to the strict management of the green's historic character by the proprietors. Even when discussing the design, placement and installation of the city's Civil War monument—arguably the most fervent moment of monument-making in all of American history—the monument committee never received permission from the proprietors, so the project never moved forward. (The City of New Haven's Soldiers' and Sailors' Monument ended up at the summit of East Rock Park instead.) The fact that the World War I Memorial Flagpole and Honor Roll was installed says two things about New Haven in the 1920s: first, that the proprietors, like everyone around them, had lived through the greatest calamity since the Civil War, and they were ready to recognize the importance of the event; second, the memorial committee was shrewd in its choice of design and placement—the New Haven Green once had a liberty pole during the American Revolution and later did have a flagpole, thus a precedence was already set. Instead of choosing a new spot on the green for a monument, the committee suggested replacing the utilitarian flagpole already in place with a grander structure built of marble and bronze. The plan worked.

Ninety tons of marble and forty tons of granite were used to build the Memorial Flagstaff and Honor Roll. The competition for the design opened to the public in 1927 and was chosen by a committee appointed by Mayor John B. Tower that included Philip H. English, a member of Company F (later M), 102nd Infantry. It was required by the committee that the "design not only combine the ideas of a War Memorial and Flagstaff but also to be in harmony with the other buildings surrounding the Green." Constructed from a design by Douglas Orr (1892–1966), the spot chosen was about twenty feet away from the flagpole but very close to the original location of the liberty pole erected during the American Revolution. The new flagpole extends eight feet into the ground for stability in weather events. The cylindrical drum was carved in low relief by Michele (or Michael) Martino, a local sculptor who worked on monuments and Works Progress Administration projects around the city, including the Spanish American War Memorial (*The Hiker*) in 1924 and the bas-relief plaques of Haggerty and Parker (see page 118). Projected to cost $30,000, the final amount came in at $44,445 when it was finished in 1929.

Above: Dedication of the World War I Memorial Flagpole and Honor Roll, New Haven, Connecticut, May 30, 1929. An ornamental base of white Georgia marble, rising to white staff, was intended to draw viewers' eyes upward to the flag, ninety-six feet in the air. The marble base is octagonal, with the names of the eight battles in which Americans fought: Chemin des Dames, Seicheprey, St. Mihiel, Château-Thierry, Marne, Aisne, Verdun and Meuse-Argonne. Seven bronze honor roll tablets with the names of the war dead were inserted on the flat sides. *Courtesy of the Connecticut State Library*.

Left: Detail of a doughboy, World War I Memorial Flagpole and Honor Roll, Douglas Orr (architect), Michele Martino (sculptor). The figures, seven feet in height, are symbolic/allegorical and directional; on the west face is a figure of war, and on the east face is a figure of peace, with the two joined together by more figures representing the different services. The ring above the figures features thirteen stars. *Photograph by William Sacco*.

The next public memorial to the Great War wasn't completed until 1937; its undertaking was due to the city's involvement with the Federal Art Project of the Works Progress Administration. The Timothy Ahearn Memorial is the only bronze monument produced in New Haven under the city's FAP/WPA program, attesting to the idealization of Ahearn as the city's war hero (see page 130). Most World War I doughboy monuments are homogenous—such as West Haven's—serving to represent all the soldiers who fought from one town or area, but the Ahearn Memorial is dedicated to one Fair Haven resident. Noted in the previous chapter, Timmy Ahearn was a member of Company C, 102nd Infantry, 26th Division, who won the Distinguished Service Cross and the *Croix de Guerre* for action at Verdun on October 17, 1918. Further, he had participated in all of the Yankee Division battles—the only New Havener with such status. The memorial provides the public script assigned to Ahearn, leaving out some important information. Two sides of the granite base are engraved with his story. Corporal Ahearn took command of his shattered unit when his commanders were killed; he then wrote a note to his superior officers on the back of a letter from his mother stating that he was "ready for any action I am called upon to perform." Later that day, Ahearn rescued a wounded officer in the face of heavy machine gun fire. What the memorial doesn't say is that after the war, Ahearn returned home to find there was no longer a job for him at the Marlin Firearms Factory. Exposure to mustard gas contributed to lingering ill health, and he became a migrant agricultural worker, dying in California in 1925, when he was not yet thirty years old. (There is some question about his birth year, 1897 or 1898.) Ahearn was buried in St. Lawrence Cemetery—not far from the bronze memorial—although few today remember his grave.

The sculpture features a heavily muscled figure typical of 1930s artwork. Dressed in a doughboy uniform, Ahearn's metal helmet is tilted to the right, and artist Karl Lang cleverly uses the base on which the statue's right leg rests to serve as a writing perch, which was also supposed to simulate a trench. The monument was the site of many Seicheprey wreath-laying ceremonies until the late 1970s, when veteran doughboys began dying from old age. Ahearn wears the YD patch on his left arm. The YD emblem is also carved on the granite base of the monument, as the New England Chapter of the YD Veterans Association instigated the commission. John T. "Jack" Dillon, Ahearn's friend at home and on the front, was chairman of the committee. The monument was originally located farther along Derby Avenue and was dedicated on Armistice Day (November 11, today Veterans Day) but was moved in 1951 when the strip of land alongside the West River became a memorial park—and members of the YD Veterans Association complained that the original placement was too remote. Although the original location for the monument was to be in a Fair Haven (also written as Fairhaven at the time) park, a World War Memorial Commission organized by George Dudley Seymour and the New Haven Board of Park Commissioners was developing a new memorial park along the West River, and thus Ahearn's statue was slated to be the first installation there. As it turns out, it would be the only bronze monument installed in the park. According to one newspaper, "[W]hile other New Haven boys have received similar decorations, the New Haven YD selected Ahearn's act as best symbolic of the YD." Of Ahearn's action, General Clarence Edwards said, "It best exemplifies the spirit of the YD."

Grave marker for Timothy Ahearn, St. Lawrence Cemetery, circa 1925. Ahearn, unlike Gilbert Nelson Jerome, was not buried with his family, and his marker stands alone, likely paid for through veterans' funds, since the plain style of marker indicates it was supplied by an organization and not selected by the family. Although today located in West Haven, St. Lawrence Cemetery was considered the Irish cemetery for New Haven in the early twentieth century. *Photograph by William Sacco.*

The women's auxiliary of the YD Post 130, American Legion, sold "Timmy Ahearn Tags," which were "small tags containing a pen sketch of the proposed memorial" at the 1937 Seicheprey observance held at the armory. In addition, Elsie Janis, the "Sweetheart of the AEF," came from her home in Beverly Hills to perform a "benefit vaudeville show" at the state armory on Goffe Street. (Philip English reported in memoirs that Janis was a "ray of sunshine, dancing for thousands of doughboys on improvised stages at a dozen fronts.") The show was preceded by a banquet dinner at the Hotel Garde, where guests, including Colonel Henry "Machine Gun" Parker, ate "roast fresh Vermont turkey a la Seicheprey" with "dressing Toul" and "candied sweet potatoes Menil-La-Tour." The following year's observance met at the monument itself.

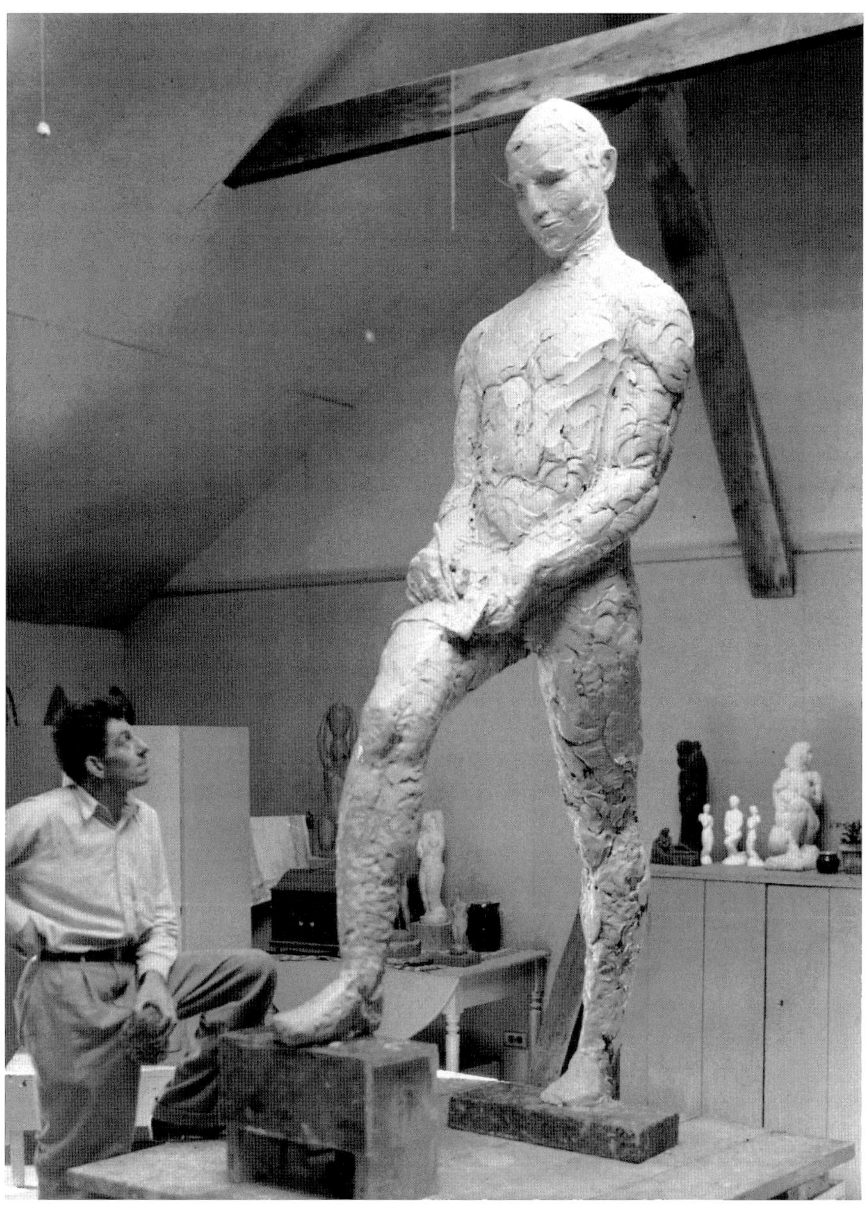

Clay maquette of the Timothy Ahearn Memorial, circa 1936–37, Noroton (Darien), Connecticut. Karl Lang's studio likely featured tall ceilings, large glass windows for light and large doors so the model could be transported. Here, Lang is shown looking up at Ahearn, showing the physical structure of the body built up in clay (likely over an armature of steel wire and/or wood) before Ahearn's uniform is shaped. The design of the monument was first worked out in small clay maquettes and then enlarged. The full-size clay maquette would then be brought to a foundry to make a mold, through which the bronze casting was done. *Courtesy of the Connecticut State Library.*

102nd Infantry Regiment Memorial, concrete, Maxwell-Pagano & Son, installed 1942, Derby Avenue, New Haven. The engraved inscription reads, "Here was organized 5 August 1917 The 102nd Infantry 26th Division United States Army Composed of Units of the 1st and 2nd Connecticut Infantry Regiments CNG This Regiment which included many sons of Yale Rendered Distinguished Service in 1918 on the Battlefields of France This tablet erected 9 August 1942 by the New Haven Chapter Yankee Division Veterans Association Aisne Marne Champagne Marne Saint Mihiel Meuse Argonne." The dedicatory address was delivered by Captain Philip H. English and Colonel Charles Lockhart, both veterans of the 102nd. *Photograph by William Sacco.*

The artist of the Timothy Ahearn Memorial was Karl Lang, who was about the same age as Ahearn, although born in Biberach, Germany, in 1897. Very poor when he came to the United States in 1914, Lang worked a series of menial jobs before becoming appointed as foreman on Gutzon Borglum's Mount Rushmore project. Lang worked for Borglum for five years before leaving to start his own studio. In addition to the Ahearn Memorial, Lang, of Darien, Connecticut, completed the *Head of Solon Kelly* for the Stamford Public Library and the Fitch Memorial in Darien. He completed the clay maquettes for the Ahearn Memorial in his studio in Noroton (Darien). The original base featured engraved images of Ahearn in motion, carved into each long side. Similar in style to the Ahearn Monument is Lang's 1936 Veterans Memorial Flagpole in Veterans Cemetery, Noroton Heights, also a WPA project. This monument was noted at the time as being "the largest individual work of art in New England financed by the Public Works of Art Project [the precursor to the Federal Art project]." Lang's work for New Haven likely supplanted that status. Family history says that Lang, who died at age fifty-five in Norwalk Hospital, suffered from a pulmonary illness brought on by exposure to dust in his studio work, an echo of the passing of Ahearn three decades earlier.

The last memorial installed to World War I in New Haven was for the 102nd Infantry Regiment itself, which continued to function after the Great War—and exists today—as an active National Guard Reserve unit. The 102nd went on to fight in World War II, and in 1942, in the midst of the next global war, members of the New Haven Chapter of the YD installed a memorial flagpole and concrete tablet. The memorial is difficult to view because it straddles two sides of the very busy Derby Avenue (where Ahearn's grave site and the bronze memorial are also located). The memorial consists of two bump-outs of brick on both sides of the street—the very street where the 102nd would march between Camp Yale and the New Haven Green. The inscribed concrete slab reminds viewers that the 102nd Regiment contained Yale men, as well as New Haven men. Earlier, in 1927, the entrance to Yale Field was decorated with the Walter Camp Memorial Gateway, a huge brick ceremonial arch.

9

YOUNG GUNS

Yale University Fights and Remembers

Yale University students, professors and alumni from across the United States joined the Allied cause in 1915 and 1916, long before the American Expeditionary Force landed in France in the fall of 1917. In the words of New Haven historian Judith Schiff, "Wartime is a catalyst for change, and many things changed at Yale." Further, "Women were coming to study the sciences, where they were needed to replace men, and the medical school opened for women." Although the university did not admit female undergraduates until 1969, women attended Yale via professional and graduate programs and served the western front in multiple capacities, including work with the American Ambulance Service attached to the YMCA, as nurses with the mobile army hospital units and as drivers for the American Field Service and the Motor Corps of America. Men of Yale often led the newest developments on the front, such as the First Yale Unit, the first naval aviation reserve regiment, formed by sophomore F. Trubee Davison in 1915. Yalies staffed army hospitals and became officers and doughboys of the infantry with both the National Guard and regular army. For example, Lieutenant Colonel Joseph Marshall Flint, professor of surgery at the Yale School of Medicine and commandant of the Yale Mobile Hospital Unit, saw seventeen months of active service. As noted in the *Yale News*, "Mobile Hospital No. 39 in the A.E.F. was staffed by Yale medical faculty and students and supported with funds from the Yale Corporation." By 1919, more than 8,000 Yalies had served, with 227 deaths, the earliest of which was First Lieutenant Arthur Bartram Randolph (class of 1906). The

"Yale in The War," *Yale Alumni Weekly*, November 23, 1917. Here two doughboys stand with the Nathan Hale Monument on Old Campus, Yale University. The statue of Hale was installed in 1914, just as the war was beginning in Europe. While members of the newly formed Yankee Division looked to the American Revolution for inspiration, Yale and New Haven looked to local hero Nathan Hale, who, at the time, was believed to have said, "I only regret that I have but one life to lose for my country." *Courtesy of Robert S. Greenberg, Made in New Haven.*

son of an American mother and a British father, Randolph joined the Welsh Guards of the British army in 1915 and was killed in September of that year. The university would remember their deaths—including Randolph's—in numerous monuments and memorials on and off campus. In the heart of downtown New Haven, the name of each Yale alumnus who died during World War I appears inside Woolsey Hall, on the white marble walls first installed to remember Civil War casualties.

On the western front, the work of Yale-associated surgeons, nurses, medics and ambulance drivers proved the university's commitment to serving the Allied cause, but this happened on the homefront as well, first, in the use of Platt, or Yale, Field for the 102nd Regiment camp, designated "Camp Yale" in "recognition of the valuable cooperation rendered the regiment by Yale University." Secondly, the university campus was used as a training ground for artillery regiments. The Yale Battery was organized in the fall of 1915 under the direction of General Leonard Wood. It rapidly grew into four batteries mustered into the Connecticut 10th Field Artillery of the National Guard. After the National Defense Act of June 3, 1916, provided for the establishment of ROTC (Reserve Officers Training Corps) units on college campuses, Yale moved to replace these militia batteries with a regular ROTC program. In the fall of 1916, with the permission of President Arthur Hadley, Yale College undergraduates began preparing for military service. Most of the young men chose artillery service, which had the greatest need. In February 1917, Lieutenant Colonel R.M. Danford, of the 302nd Regiment of Field Artillery, came to Yale to train the students, using the school's baseball batting cages, the Orange Street Armory and Old Campus for drills and Osborne Hall for the classroom. The result of this public display of higher education's dedication to the war effort resulted in the arrival of four 75-millimeter guns with caissons, sent to campus by France when the Americans joined the war in the spring of 1917.

The Guns, thank God for Yale and the Guns!

—Lieutenant Colonel Robert M. Danford, head of artillery instruction at Yale College

Yale offered a series of "complete military training courses" for artillery officers overseen by Captain W.S. Overton, a retired army officer; a "quartet of the famous French 75's"; and Captain A.G. Bland and Lieutenant R.H. Massey of the Canadian Field Artillery, who had already seen service in France. Yale University contributed Professor E.B. Reed, who prepared for his

Base Hospital, No. 1, from the *War Series*, George Bellows, lithograph, 1918. Bellows, an American artist known today as part of the Ashcan School of New York, volunteered for the tank division of the U.S. Army in 1917. He did not see active service on the front but was affected by the rumors—some documented—of German atrocities against civilians in Belgium in 1914. Over the course of a year and a half, Bellows created a series of lithographs, drawings and oil paintings, including this one, of medical staff working on a soldier in the shadows of a village church. *Courtesy of the Yale University Art Gallery.*

Memorial Rotunda, Woolsey Hall, Yale University, Hans Hering, installed 1913–15. The origin of Yale's first Civil War memorial was based in the university's attempt to reconcile northern and southern division during Reconstruction. But it took the university decades to move the project forward. After its installation, which features four allegorical figures in bas-relief (*Peace*, *Devotion*, *Memory* and *Courage*) with the names of the dead, the memorial continued to grow, with the addition of names, units of service and location and date of death from the world wars and then Korea and Vietnam. *Photograph by William Sacco.*

work at the U.S. School of Fire at Fort Sill in the summer of 1917. Yale was also promised two mountain guns and horses by the War Department. Hotel Taft was used to house the regular army officers—captains and lieutenants—who came to the city to train soldiers. Osborne Hall continued to function as the site for lecture courses for the ROTC, Scoutmasters and others from the Boy Scouts through 1919.

It was Yale's thinking that university students entered the university at age eighteen and wanted training so that by graduation at age twenty-one, they were prepared to enter military service as an officer. Four years of coursework was condensed into three during the war years through the ROTC and was particularly suited to students at Yale's Sheffield Scientific School (as noted in chapter 1, Gilbert Nelson Jerome graduated from Sheffield), although the ROTC course was open to Yale college students as well. Yale ROTC students were given instruction in artillery, mathematics, surveying, cartography, navigation and trigonometry as well as geology, the history of American international relations, European diplomatic history, French and the physical sciences. Particular to the artillery, handling big guns included working with camouflage, gun positions and ammunition. The *New Haven Register* reported on November 18, 1917:

> *One of the highest compliments that has ever been paid to Yale University is that which the United States government paid when it decided to send its regular officers to this city in order that they might obtain what really amounts to a finishing education in the matter of artillery. It practically amounts to an acknowledgment that nowhere in the country is there a place where the art of teaching the finer points of the big guns can be so perfectly as here in New Haven and at Yale.*

In addition to the ROTC program, the Yale Naval Training Unit (originally the Motor Boat Patrol) was also officially organized at this time under the direction of Mather Abbott. The unit also helped in the preparation for navy examinations for those wishing to become ensigns. A naval training course was offered by men who had been on the Yale training vessel *Ansantawae* the summer before. (*Ansantawae* is the name of a Native American chief from nearby Milford, Connecticut, on Long Island Sound.) In his work, Abbot, was assisted by H.L. Seward and Clarence Mendell. The three-year course was again opened to Yale College students as well as Sheffield Scientific School students. Elementary navigation and seamanship, signaling, ordnance and gunnery and nautical astronomy were part of the curriculum.

Yale University also helped civilians in New Haven and Connecticut serve the war front. Captain F.W. Cook and Lieutenant Henry R. Congdon, assistants to the commandant at Yale University, were available to help civilians interested in applying for admission to officer training schools. Their office was located at 10 Fayerweather Hall and responsible for infantry, coast (heavy) artillery, field artillery and machine gun schools. An advertisement from their office read, "[M]en of character and intelligence and particularly men of maturity and experience, are desired for these camps. The Army has a particular need at this time for good Officers." Lieutenant John K. Murphy of Yale University, a reservist in the navy, was in charge of

> *For God, for Country, for Yale.*
>
> *—Harkness Memorial Gateway, 1922*

the territory between New London and Bridgeport, working from an office at 88 High Street. The munitions plants at both New Haven and Bridgeport, located close to Long Island Sound, were of interest and needed surveillance for safety. In case of an emergency, Murphy would oversee private citizens wishing to use their boats to assist the government.

As noted, it wasn't just Yale students and graduates who went to war—professors also left their posts to enlist, such as Professor Charles Bakewell of the philosophy department, who flew with the air squadron in 1917. In 1918, he became an inspector with the Italian Red Cross and was assigned to Italy to survey war damage and work on reconstruction. Likewise, Hiram Bingham III, a Yale graduate and professor already famous for his "discovery" of Machu Picchu in 1911, became a captain in the Connecticut National Guard in 1916 and then—using his past experiences in surveying archaeological sites—became an aviator, eventually organizing the U.S. Schools of Military Aeronautics across the country through the aviation section of the U.S. Signal Corps and managing a flying program at

Yale Alumni War Memorial, Thomas Hastings and Everett V. Meeks, sandstone and slate, 1926–27, Hewitt Memorial Quardrangle. Described as an "altar to liberty" by the university, traditional victory images of eagles and laurel wreaths are interspersed with tanks, guns and other machines of World War I, the first war to use modern technology. Hastings had earlier completed the Ledyard Flagstaff Memorial, a flagpole to the Spanish-American War, but here he was joined by art professor Everett V. Meeks, making this a unique statement of Yale war history. *Courtesy of Yale University.*

Postcard, Memorial Colonnade, Hewitt Memorial Quadrangle. *Author's collection.*

Issoudon, France (where Gilbert Nelson Jerome had trained). At least one professor, John Duer Irving, of the geology department and a captain in the Engineers' Corps, died on July 20, 1918.

Yale's involvement with artillery training is almost forgotten today, although a visual record of it exists on the Yale Alumni War Memorial on Hewitt Quadrangle. A resolution was passed by the memorial committee in 1919 and paid for by alumni. A cenotaph design was chosen, echoing the cenotaph erected at Whitehall in London on November 11, 1920. London's version—which began as a temporary plaster for a peace parade but was replaced to become the country's primary World War I monument—features an unadorned four-sided vertical block against which flags stand. Yale's cenotaph, in contrast, is covered in images that reinforce the machines of war. The project was expanded to include carvings of the names of the major American-fought battles of the war by adding a Classical colonnade onto the hall. The memorial committee wanted the monument to "express the sentiment of the Alumni, rather than serve any utilitarian purpose" and to "instill into the minds of our youth, to new generations of leaders, the duty and glory of sacrifice and a steadying knowledge of our best traditions." As much as $150,000 was allocated for the design and construction, making it one of the most expensive public art projects in New Haven to that date.

10
NEW HAVEN WORLD WAR I MEMORIAL ROLL, 1917–1919

American troops saw action for barely more than a year with the American Expeditionary Force (AEF) in Europe, suffering just over 53,400 dead, 204,000 wounded and 63,114 noncombat deaths. Only the Civil War and World War II produced more American casualties over longer periods of time. The ongoing war in Afghanistan is the longest war Americans have been involved in to date, but the numbers of war dead are much smaller. The following men and women from New Haven were killed in action or died from wounds, disease or accidents during the Great War. Several memorial rolls exist with discrepancies between them, but all names have been included here, with as much information as to status, service and date of death as possible. When reading through the memorial roll, it is possible to see patterns—such as the number of machine gunners who perished and the 17 Company C and Company D soldiers of the 102nd Regiment, 26th Yankee Division, from New Haven who died together on April 20, 1918, near Seicheprey, France—one of the first attacks by Germans on the American military in World War I. In total, 84 New Haven men died as Yankee Division soldiers. But knowledge also surfaces that no one is safe on the front during wartime. Infantry soldiers and machine gunners died, but so, too, did buglers, farriers, sailors, wagoners, cooks, engineers, boiler makers, supply clerks, photographers, ambulance drivers and nurses. Rank was also not a safety net, as sergeants, corporals, lieutenants, captains and majors all died, although not in equal numbers.

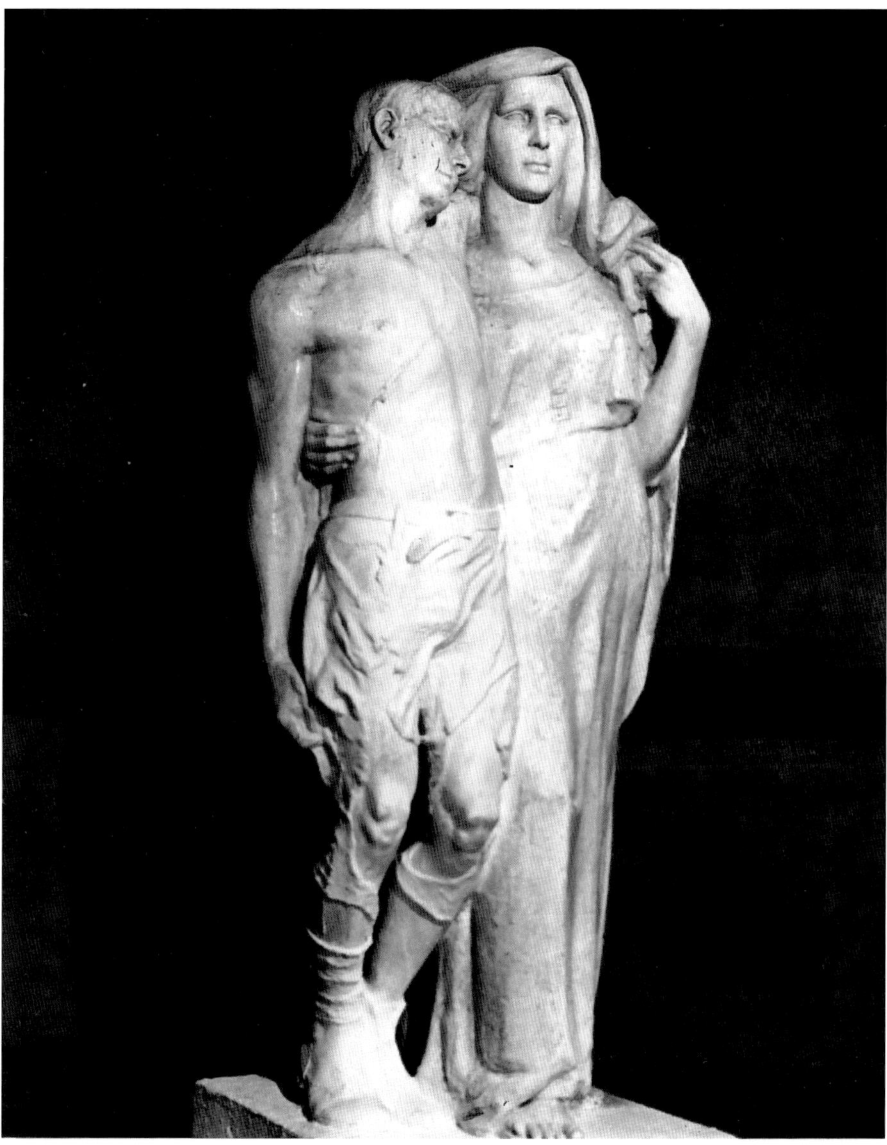

Guardsmen Memorial, Salvatore M. Milici, marble, circa 1936. Milici was born in New Haven and attended Truman School. He dropped out of New Haven High School to earn a living and attended YMCA night school before earning a scholarship to the Yale School of Fine Arts. During the 1930s, the artist was on the WPA art rolls, completing several art projects for the armory on Goffe Street. Milici, who lived at 215 Henry Street, carved this statue during his tenure studying at Yale. He donated this sculpture to the 102nd Infantry, which placed it in the armory as a memorial to guardsmen. *Courtesy of the Connecticut State Library.*

By their acts their names are indelibly inscribed upon the annals of American history their glory is immortal—part and parcel of the glorious history of America and the world. We cannot add luster to their memory.

—Soldiers of the Great War, Volume I, *1920*

The first New Havener to die in World War I was Corporal Horace Foulds of the American Expeditionary Force. Before enlisting, Foulds boarded at 123 Congress Avenue with Mrs. M. Shepard, as his own mother lived in England. Four members of his family were serving with the Allies. He was a member of the local Bricklayers' Union and, not surprisingly, also a member of New Haven's British-American Club, which draped its headquarters in mourning bunting (much as the Jerome family would do in the living room of their house) after learning of Foulds's death. The New Haven newspapers that reported his death in 1917 did not know where or how Foulds was wounded, but he later died in a field hospital "back of the lines." His death on November 25, 1917, made him one of the earliest casualties of the war for Americans, since the AEF did not reach the front en masse until February of the following year.

Soldiers who enlisted or were drafted were listed on New Haven's "honor roll," which appeared in city newspapers. The Elm City lost more than 261 men and 2 women—Irene M. Flynn and Helen A. Moakley, both nurses with the American Red Cross—all of whose names then became part of the "memorial roll." Of the war dead, at least three New Haveners earned the Distinguished Service Cross and another man the *Croix de Guerre* (war cross) from France. One man, Russell Drury with the 102nd Field Hospital, earned both. Their awards are highlighted in bold text. Many soldiers on the western front who earned these awards survived the war, including John Dillon and Timothy Ahearn, friends from Fair Haven and both of the 102nd Regiment. The last statewide gathering of Yankee Division World War I veterans—gathered into groups called "barracks"—was in 1983 in Milford.

The names and associated information came from multiple sources, including *Soldiers of the Great War, Volume I*, 1920, the program for the Dedication of the World War Memorial and Honor Roll, New Haven Green, May 30, 1929, and the "List of Connecticut Soldiers Who Died in France," compiled by the Soldiers Record Publishing Company in Washington, D.C., and arranged alphabetically by Charles Hale for the Connecticut State Library in 1931.

Out from Battle, Wallace Morgan, charcoal on paper sketch, 1918. *Courtesy of the National Museum of American History, Smithsonian Institution.*

Amarante, Matthew (Private), died of disease, date unknown

Amato, John (Private, Company I, 325th Infantry), d. September 22, 1918

Anzalone, Frank (Company M, 113th Infantry), d. October 11, 1918

Ashford, Frederick (Private, 1st class, Company E, 102nd Infantry), d. November 20, 1918

Asprelli, Valentine (Private), died of disease, date unknown

Baker, John Russell (4th Recruit Company, General Services Infantry), d. October 4, 1918

Barnes, Frederick T. (Sergeant, Company K, 84th Infantry), d. October 4, 1918

Bartlett, Harry B. (Company D, 103rd Machine Gun Battalion), d. April 27, 1918

Beauton, Joseph Emmet (First Lieutenant, 140th Aero Squadron, Signal Corps), d. June 3, 1918

Bennett, Elmer J. (Company C, 3rd Battalion, Edgewood Arsenal, Maryland), d. October 16, 1918

Berger, Elwood D. (Corporal, Company D, 102nd Infantry), d. April 20, 1918

Bernstein, George J. (Corporal, Ordnance Department), d. January 28, 1919

Bews, Joseph N. (Corporal, Motor Transport Corps), d. March 10, 1919

Bimbo, Arthur (Private), killed in action, date unknown

Blumberg, Harris (Private, Medical Detachment, 28th Infantry), d. September 23, 1918

Bohan, John F. (Chief Gunner's Mate, U.S. Navy), d. March 19, 1919

Boldt, Herman St. John, Jr. (First Lieutenant, Air Service), d. July 20, 1918

Boswell, Jonathan (First Quebec Regiment, Black Watch, British Army), d. September 29, 1918

Bothwell, Donald C. (42nd Highlanders, Black Watch, British Army), d. September 2, 1918

Boylan, Walter J. (Corporal, Quartermaster's Corps), d. December 3, 1918

Braden, Joseph F. (Sergeant, Company B, 102nd Infantry), d. October 25, 1918

Bradford, Fred James (Private, Company A, 39th Infantry), d. October 19, 1918

Bradley, William J. (Private, 1st Class, Company F, 102nd Infantry), d. October 23, 1918

Brady, Philip J. (Private or Sergeant, Company C, 102nd Infantry), d. April 20, 1918

Brandolini, Vincenzo (Private, Battery F, 74th Field Artillery), d. February 18, 1919

Breen, Denis (Private, Company G, 58th Infantry), d. December 10, 1918

Brennan, John J. (Corporal, Company B, 102nd Infantry), d. July 25, 1918

Brereton, John J. (Private, Company F, 58th Infantry), d. October 10, 1918

Brewster, Albert A. (1st Class Seaman, U.S. Navy), d. September 19, 1918

Brode, Robert L. (17th Company, 5th Battalion, Camp Devens), d. May 4, 1918

Broder, John V. (Private, Company H, 127th Infantry), d. February 12, 1919

Brown, James C. (Private), died of disease, date unknown

Bruce, Robert J. (Corporal, Troop D, 2nd Cavalry), d. December 23, 1918

Buckley, Charles T. (Private, First Lieutenant, Air Service), d. September 25, 1918

Buckner, Paul (Private, Corporal, Company M, 372nd Infantry), d. September 26, 1918

Burns, James J. (Private, Battery D, 305th Field Artillery), d. February 10, 1919

Burro, Frank (Company D, 9th Ammunition Train), d. October 19, 1918

Bush, Louis W. (Commissary Steward, U.S. Navy), d. October 3, 1918

Butler, Richard F. (Private, Company D, 102nd Machine Gun Battalion), d. September 16, 1918
***Distinguished Service Cross**

Butterfield, William J. (Company H, 115th Infantry), d. October 18, 1918

Callahan, Daniel F. (Private, Company D, 102nd Machine Gun Battalion), d. July 22, 1918

Cantwell, James Edward (Lieutenant, Company D, 101st Machine Gun Battalion), d. October 16, 1918

Cappiello, Michael (Sergeant, Company B, 102nd Infantry), d. July 23, 1918

Cappuccio, Alphonso (Private, Bugler, 102nd Infantry Machine Gun Company), d. November 5, 1918

Ruins of Seicheprey, Ernest Clifford Piexotto, charcoal on paper, circa 1918. *Courtesy of the National Museum of American History, Smithsonian Institution.*

Carbonelli, Angelo (Private, Company D, 9th Infantry), d. September 12, 1918
Card, George F. (Sergeant, Battery F, 302nd Field Artillery), d. February 6, 1919
Carroll, Joseph P. (Seaman, U.S. Navy), d. January 6, 1919
Cavallero, Angelo (Company D, 103rd Machine Gun Battalion), d. January 31, 1919
Cerulo, Luigi (Private, Company B, 102nd Infantry), d. July 23, 1918
Chamberlain, Earle Holmes (Corporal, 55th Company, 5th Regiment Marine Corps), d. October 9, 1918
Chernin, Max (301st Water Tank Train), d. August 15, 1918
Chung, Wailing (23rd Company, 152nd Depot Brigade), d. May 14, 1918
Church, Lester H. (Seaman, U.S. Navy), d. September 26, 1918
Clinton, Harry L. (Company L, 304th Infantry), d. September 10, 1918
Cole, Alfred B. (Private, Mechanic, Company B, 102nd Infantry), d. August 2, 1918
Collins, Maurice (Private, Company D, 60th Infantry), d. October 14, 1918
Conase, Ernest (Wagoner, Supply Company, 102nd Infantry), d. September 20, 1917
Condon, Edward J. (Private, Company E, 102nd Infantry), d. December 14, 1917
Cooper, George H. (Company C, 102nd Infantry), d. April 20, 1918
Cort, Thomas L. (First Company, Camp Raritan, N.J.), d. August 31, 1918
Costello, Frank, Jr. (Private, Company F, Evacuation Hospital Group 51), d. October 13, 1918
Cox, Henry F. (Battery E, 302nd Field Artillery), d. October 6, 1918
Craven, William S. (Cook, Section 577, American Ambulance Service), d. April 25, 1918
Crawford, William T. (53rd Company, 151st Depot Brigade), d. November 2, 1918
Creamer, Francis T. (Troop A, 8th Cavalry), d. November 12, 1918
Crocco, Joseph (Private), killed in action, date unknown
Cummings, Leonard J. (Private, 320th Machine Gun Battalion), d. October 17, 1918
Dadzinski, John S. (Company B, 164th Infantry), d. November 4, 1918
Daly, Henry T. (20th Sanitary Train), d. October 5, 1918
Danielak, Stanley (Private), died of disease, date unknown

Daniels, William A. (Sergeant, Company M, 372nd Infantry), d. October 21, 1918

Darcy, John P. (Private, Company C, 102nd Infantry), d. April 20, 1918

Darling, William H. (Company B, 102nd Infantry), d. February 2, 1918

***First New Havener of the 102nd Regiment to die in action**

Darrow, Charles Wesley (Company D, 102nd Infantry), d. April 20, 1918

Dedrick, Eugene B. (Chief Boatswain's Mate, U.S. Navy), d. February 26, 1919

DeForrest, Clinton W. (Private or Corporal, Company C, 102nd Infantry), d. April 20, 1918

DeFreese, Henry (Captain, U.S. Infantry), d. November 10, 1917

Deskin, George F. (Private, 106th Field Artillery), d. October 9, 1918

Dippold, Henry P. (Supply Company, 102nd Infantry), d. September 18, 1918

Dohna, Alfred (Private, Battery E, 103rd Field Artillery), d. September 23, 1918

Dole, George D. (Corporal, Company B, 102nd Infantry), d. June 13, 1918

Donahue, Eugene J. (2nd Company, 7th Canadian Infantry Battalion), d. September 9, 1916

Donahue, Joseph C. (Company D, 102nd Infantry), d. July 23, 1918

Donnarummo, Anthony (status unknown) killed in action, date unknown

Dosch, George Conrad (Company A, 26th Infantry), d. October 7, 1918

Drury, Russell (Ambulance Driver, 102nd Field Hospital), d. February 5, 1919

*** Distinguished Service Cross, *Croix de Guerre***

Duffy, Charles F. (Private, 19th U.S. Engineers), d. June 13, 1918

Edwards, Raymond W. (Private), died of disease, date unknown

Erickson, Leonard E. (Company E, 102nd Infantry), d. July 27, 1918

Falvey, Daniel J. (Company E, 314th Infantry), d. September 30, 1918

Farrell, Bernard (Private, Battery B, 13th Field Artillery), d. September 28, 1918

Farrell, Charles F. (Private, 302nd Machine Gun Battalion), d. March 11, 1919

These men, the flower of New Haven's youth, went gladly from their homes at their country's call eager to do their duty for the commonwealth…with no thoughts of self, no fear under the shadow of death, no other belief than that right is might.

—newspaper headline, "Six of New Haven's Most Gallant War Heroes to Be Buried This Week," 1921

FARRELL, PAUL R. (Sergeant, Company B, 102nd Infantry), d. July 21, 1918
FAST, HARRY (Private, Company L, 18th Infantry), d. October 4, 1918
FIORILLO, AMADEO (Private, 1st Class, Company A, 9th Infantry), d. November 4, 1918
FITZPATRICK, JOHN D. (Private, Company D, 102nd Infantry), d. April 20, 1918
FLAHERTY, CHRISTOPHER T. (Private, Company F, 102nd Infantry), d. October 23, 1918
FLANNERY, THOMAS F. (Boilermaker, U.S. Navy), d. February 7, 1919
FLORIAN, ADAM (3rd Development Battalion, Camp Devens), d. September 26, 1918
FLYNN, IRENE M. (Nurse, American Red Cross), d. July 13, 1918
FOLEY, JOHN JAMES (Private, Company H, 314th Infantry), d. November 7, 1918
FOLEY, MATTHEW J. (First Lieutenant, Medical Corps), d. October 10, 1918
FORD, EDWARD L. (Lieutenant, Company G, 23rd Infantry), d. July 18, 1918
Croix de Guerre
FOSTER, ALLEN G. (Private, 37th Provisional Ordnance Detachment), d. September 15, 1918
FOULDS, HORACE (Corporal, Headquarters Company, 23rd Infantry), d. November 25, 1917
***First New Havener to die in World War I**
FOX, THOMAS (Private, Company B, 314th Infantry), d. November 1, 1918
FRANCIS, JOSEPH (Company C, 102nd Infantry), d. April 20, 1918
FRANZ, ARTHUR (Company C, 102nd Infantry), d. April 20, 1918
FREELAND, GEORGE C. (Captain, Company D, 102nd Infantry), d. October 1, 1918
FREITAG, FRANK X. (Private, Company B, 305th Infantry), d. September 27, 1918
FRIEND, RAYMOND E. (Company M, 50th Infantry), d. January 20, 1919
GALLIVER, HARRY K. (U.S. Navy), d. July 25, 1918
GALVIN, JOHN J. (Private), killed in action, date unknown
GEHRKE, WILLIAM F. (Company E, 102nd Infantry), d. September 18, 1917
GELENEAU, GEORGE J. (Sergeant, Company C, 102nd Infantry), d. July 23, 1918
GIAMARCO, ANGELO (Company M, 26th Infantry), d. October 12, 1918
GIANOTTI, GIUSEPPI (Company L, 102nd Infantry), d. July 21, 1918
GOGGINS, JAMES L. (Lieutenant, Quartermaster's Department, Aviation Section), d. August 11, 1918

Goodwin, Victor Francis (Battery D, 76th Field Artillery), d. November 10, 1918

Gordon, Frank P. (Private, 1st Class, Battery F, 103rd Field Artillery), d. April 20, 1918

***Distinguished Service Cross**

Gray, Edward D. (Company D, 102nd Infantry), d. October 15, 1918

Gritzback, George (Corporal, Company C, 102nd Infantry), d. April 20, 1918

Gruettke, William (Private, Company G, 328th Infantry), d. October 14, 1918

Gunn, Leon L. (Private, Company G, 28th Infantry), d. October 26, 1918

Hackett, James A. (Corporal, 45th Company, 12th Battalion Depot Brigade), d. September 21, 1918

Hackett, Roger (Fireman, U.S. Navy), d. August 7, 1918

***First New Havener to die abroad and brought back home for burial (killed in explosion at sea)**

Hale, E. Carleton (Quartermaster, U.S. Navy), d. September 21, 1918

Hall, Frederick A. (Corporal, Company G, 102nd Infantry), d. October 24, 1918

Hall, Herbert H. (Company D, 102nd Infantry), d. October 7, 1918

Halley, Clarence A. (Private), died of disease, date unknown

Halligan, William Clarence (Private, 308th Infantry), d. October 7, 1918

Halpin, James L. (Sergeant, Company H, 326th Infantry), d. October 24, 1918

Hanley, Alfred J. (Private, Company D, 102nd Infantry), d. April 20, 1918

Harvey, Daniel J. (Corporal, Company M, 38th Infantry), d. July 1, 1918

Hawley, Clarence A. (Company M, 372nd Infantry), d. September 23, 1918

Healey, John B. (Private), killed in action, date unknown

***Healey falsified his papers and entered the war at age sixteen**

Heery, Nichols W. (Company H, 319th Infantry), d. September 26, 1918

Hemingway, Harold Ludington (Lieutenant, Company F and K, 104th Infantry), d. October 21, 1918

***Distinguished Service Cross**

Hemingway, William H. (Private, Company B, 113th Infantry), d. October 25, 1918

Hesse, Theodore (Private, Company D, 102nd Infantry), d. April 20, 1918

Higgins, Edward (British army), date unknown

Higgins, Nicholas (Private)

Higgins, Nicholas (Company A, 70th Infantry), d. July 20, 1918
***Nicholas and Edward were brothers living at 30 Fox Street; both buried in France**

Hitchcock, Nelson (Fireman, U.S. Navy), d. June 14, 1918
Hodes, Meyer (Private, Company D, 316th Infantry), d. October 29, 1918
Hogan, William F. (Cook, Camp Meade, Maryland), d. October 14, 1918
Hotchkiss, Harold (Private), killed in action, date unknown
Irving, John Duer (Captain, U.S. Engineers), d. July 26, 1918
Jay, Michael (Private, Company I, 102nd Infantry), d. June 11, 1918
Jeanett, Mario (Private, Company I, 9th Infantry), d. July 16, 1918
Jerome, Gilbert Nelson (First Lieutenant, Aviation Section, Escadrille Spad 90), d. July 12, 1918
Johnson, Albert E. (First Lieutenant, Company C, 102nd Infantry), d. May 8, 1918
Johnson, Harley T. (Private), died of wounds, date unknown
Johnson, James H. (Corporal), killed in action, date unknown
Joyce, James N. (Private, Company C, 102nd Infantry), d. April 20, 1918
Kadelski, Stanley (Private, Company B, 102nd Infantry), d. July 23, 1918
Kaiser, Thomas (Private), died of wounds, date unknown

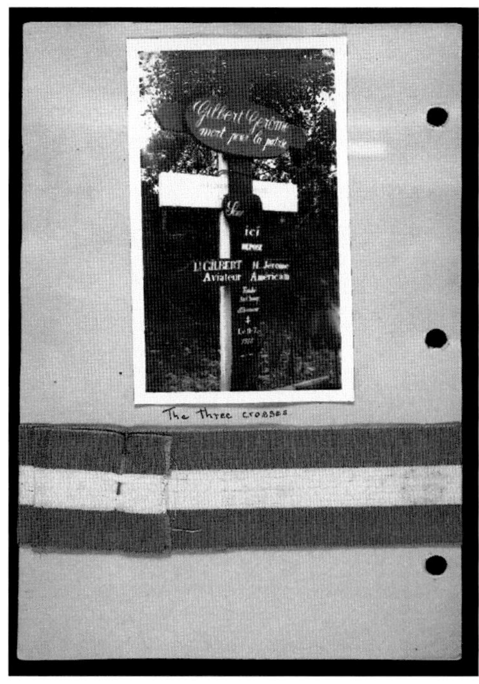

Gilbert Nelson Jerome crosses at Blâmont, France, 1918. One Frenchmen wrote of American soldiers, "[S]everal of your comrades lie at rest in our truly Christian and French soil. Their ashes shall be cared for as if they were our own." This page is from Jennie's scrapbook of her travels to France in 1919 with her mother to visit places of Gilbert's life and death. *Courtesy of the Mount Holyoke College Archives and Special Collections.*

Detail of a doughboy, Harkness Memorial Gateway, Samuel Yellin, High Street, Yale University, 1918–22. Several New Haven residents were also Yale students or alumni, including Gilbert Nelson Jerome and Harold Ludington Hemingway, therefore their names appear on memorials for both the city and the university. *Photograph by William Sacco.*

Kanoff, Raymond (Private, Company C, 102nd Regiment), d. April 20, 1918
Kaufman, Mitchell (Private, Cook, Company C, 166th Infantry), d. October 12, 1918
Kearney, Kenneth M. (Cadet, Royal Flying Corps), d. February 3, 1918
Kennedy, William J. (Private, 1st Class, Company D, 102nd Machine Gun Battalion), d. October 3, 1918
Kilcran, Joseph Patrick (Company G, 316th Infantry), d. August 3, 1918
Killeen, James C. (Private), killed in action, date unknown
Kiloren, Joseph (Private), died of disease, date unknown
Klingebiel, William J. (Private, Company D, 103rd Machine Gun Battalion), d. April 27, 1918
Knight, Joseph P. (Private, 1st Class, Battery B, 302nd Field Artillery), d. November 1, 1918
Kolodzeonzyk, Alexander (Private, Company B, 102nd Infantry), d. July 23, 1918
Langan, Edwin J. (Lieutenant, 13th Aero Squadron), d. December 13, 1918
Lawrence, Walter Edward, Jr. (Hospital Apprentice, U.S. Navy), d. July 16, 1918
Lee, Burton M. (Seaman, U.S. Navy), d. June 19, 1918
Lee, John Thomas (Private, Company E, 320th Machine Gun Battalion), d. October 16, 1918
Leigh, Charles B. (Private, Company I, 18th Infantry), d. July 18, 1918
Leonard, William F. (Private, Battery B, 321st Field Artillery), d. November 2, 1918
Lilley, John E. (Private, Company C, 102nd Infantry), d. April 20, 1918
Lucas, Clarence Nelson (Company L, 40th Infantry), d. October 11, 1918
Lund, Eric F. (Company E, 316th Infantry), d. October 14, 1918

Trench art, embossed and engraved brass munitions casings. Trench art was made as souvenirs either by soldiers at the front, by those civilians living around the front or by commercial companies for purchase by soldiers. Today, there remain millions of tons of unexploded ordnance and metal parts all along the western front. The flower patterns and shiny surfaces of these "ambiguous works of art" belie their original deadly intent. The shell casing at the left is inscribed "Chateau Thierry 1918" and the one at the right, "Verdun T.T.H." (or J.J.H.). *Courtesy of the West Haven Veterans Museum & Learning Center.*

MacArthur, William M. (Private, Company D, 103rd Machine Gun Battalion), d. October 23, 1918

Martino, John C. (Motor Company 4, Medical Corps), d. October 10, 1918

Mayo, Michael (Corporal, U.S. Army), d. April 19, 1917

McAviney, Justin I. (Private, Company D, 102nd Machine Gun Battalion), d. May 31, 1918

McCabe, James T. (Private, Company I, 61st Infantry), d. October 14, 1918

McCluskey, William (Private, Company D, 316th Infantry), d. November 7, 1918

McDermott, John F. (Corporal, Company B, 102nd Infantry), d. April 9, 1918

McGowan, John (Seaman, U.S. Navy), d. October 16, 1918

McGrath, Thomas H. (Private, Company I, 320th Infantry), d. August 14, 1918

MCNAMARA, JOHN (Private), died of accident, date unknown
MCNERNEY, MICHAEL J. (Private, Company I, 23rd Infantry), d. July 1, 1918
MCNULTY, JOSEPH P. (Private, Company G, 316th Infantry), d. September 28, 1918
MEICKLE, WILLIAM N., JR. (Company D, 103rd Machine Gun Battalion), d. November 14, 1918
MENDILLO, FRANK J. (Private, Company C, 102nd Infantry), d. April 20, 1918
MERWIN, JOHN JULIAN (Radio Landsman, U.S. Navy), d. April 10, 1918
MERWIN, THOMAS J. (Private, Company D, 316th Infantry), d. October 9, 1918
MIDAS, ALEXANDER (Private, Company E, 9th Infantry), d. October 2, 1918
MILONE, ALFONSO (Company D, 305th Infantry), d. October 7, 1918
MITCHELL, ROBERT E. (Private, 7th Company, 302nd Depot Brigade), d. June 6, 1918
MOAKLEY, HELEN A. (Nurse, American Red Cross), d. August 22, 1918
MOLAMPY, BERNARD T. (Wagoner, Battery F, 302nd Field Artillery), d. February 4, 1919
MOONEY, THOMAS J. (23rd Company, 6th Development Battalion, 154th Depot Brigade), d. October 3, 1918
MORGAN, GEORGE R. (Company E, 318th Telephone Battalion, Signal Corps), d. July 29, 1918
MORIARTY, THOMAS J. (Company A, 9th Mounted Engineers), d. March 10, 1919
MOSHER, CYRIL (Sergeant), died of wounds, date unknown
MULLEN, TERRENCE (Ordnance Detachment, Advance Ordnance Depot), d. December 30, 1918
MURRAY, WILLIAM J. (Company L, 102nd Infantry), d. October 3, 1918
MYLOTT, GEORGE E. (Company D, 47th Infantry), d. August 3, 1918
NEERY, NICHOLAS W. (U.S. Army), date of death unknown
NETTLETON, FRANK A. (Corporal, Quartermaster Corps), d. May 3, 1919
NEWMAN, JOHN J. (Troop B, 7th Cavalry), d. October 14, 1918
NORGI, SALVATORE (Private, Machine Gun Company, 102nd Infantry), d. December 26, 1918
NYREN, ROBERT C. (Seaman, U.S. Navy), d. October 5, 1918
OBERLE, PAUL (Corporal, Blacksmith, Motor Section, 5th Army Corps Artillery), d. November 12, 1918
OBERMAN, LOUIS (Corporal, Company D, 102nd Infantry), d. April 20, 1918
O'BRIEN, JAMES T. (Corporal, Medical Corps), d. January 2, 1919

O'Donnell, Thomas F. (Corporal, Company F, 5th Infantry), d. October 13, 1918

O'Grady, John J. (Private), died of wounds, date unknown

Page, Howard Edward (Battery E, 103rd Field Artillery), d. January 22, 1919

Palermo, Nicholas (Private, Battery A, 16th Field Artillery), d. July 18, 1918

Pape, Arthur R. (Private, 1st Class, Company E, 316th Infantry), d. October 12, 1918

They wrote in the old days that it is sweet and fitting to die for one's country. But in modern war there is nothing sweet, nor fitting in your dying. You will die like a dog for no good reason.

—*Ernest Hemingway,* Notes on the Next War: A Serious Topical Letter, *1935*

Pappis, Vassilios (Company C, 110th Infantry), d. September 29, 1919

Parmelee, Arthur O. (Private), died of wounds, date unknown

Parrell, Joseph F. (Company A, 316th Infantry), d. September 26, 1918

Paton, John A. (Lieutenant or Captain, Company D, 102nd Machine Gun Battalion), d. October 27, 1918

Paulay, Joseph (Private, Company H, 9th Infantry), d. July 2, 1918

Pawline, Thomas (Corporal, Battery E, 103rd Field Artillery), d. May 14, 1919

Pluff, Nelson A. (Private, Company C, 102nd Infantry), d. May 28, 1918

Polverari, Mario (Private, 1st Class, Quartermaster Corps), d. October 15, 1918

Potter, Burton (Company F, 102nd Infantry), d. May 23, 1918

Puorto, Ciro (Company G, 316th Infantry), d. October 30, 1918

Reader, Alfred W. (2nd Class Carpenter's Mate, U.S. Navy), d. January 18, 1918

Remington, Robert B. (Headquarters Company, 102nd Infantry), d. May 1, 1918

Rentschler, Fred Jacob (Private, Company D, 102nd Infantry), d. July 22, 1918

Richitelli, Joseph (Jay) (Private, Company B, 102nd Infantry), d. July 23, 1918

Rogers, Charles Lyon, III (Lieutenant, 102nd Machine Gun Battalion), d. November 8, 1918

Romano, Michael (Private, 1st Class, Company M, 116th Infantry), d. October 9, 1918

Rosencrans, William C. (U.S. Navy), d. September 16, 1918
Rosenthal, Samuel (Private), died of disease, date unknown
Rubin, Joseph A. (Quartermaster's Corps, Fort Slocum, NY), d. October 23, 1918
Ruckelshausen, Frederick E. (Mechanic, Company E, 102nd Infantry), d. May 8, 1918
Ruff, Walter H. (Army Postal Service, Washington, D.C.), d. September 22, 1918
Russell, Dwight C. (Master Mechanic, 2nd Class, U.S. Navy), d. April 13, 1918
Salvator, Nicholas (Private), killed in action, date unknown
Santaniello, Frank (Battery F, 302nd Field Artillery), d. October 10, 1918
Scandone, Peter (Photo Section, Aero Service), d. August 2, 1918
Schalina, Lawrence L. (Cook, Battery E, 103rd Field Artillery), d. November 5, 1918
Schmitz, Henry J. (Company F, 102nd Infantry), d. July 21, 1918
Schulze, Delbert E. (Seaman, U.S. Navy), d. December 5, 1918
Seufert, Frank A. (Battery A, 310th Field Artillery), d. September 26, 1918
Shanley, Peter J. (U.S. Navy), d. October 8, 1918
Sillivan, Jeremiah Russell (Company B, 102nd Infantry), d. July 22, 1918
Sillivan, John J. (Headquarters Company, 327th Infantry), d. August 12, 1918
Simmons, Chester (17th Battery, 151st Depot Brigade), d. April 7, 1918
Socia, Arthur L. (Private, Company D, 102nd Infantry), d. July 23, 1918
Croix de Guerre
Spencer, James C. (Private), killed in action, date unknown
Sproul, Thomas J. (37th Company, 10th Training Battalion. 151st Deport Brigade), d. October 5, 1918

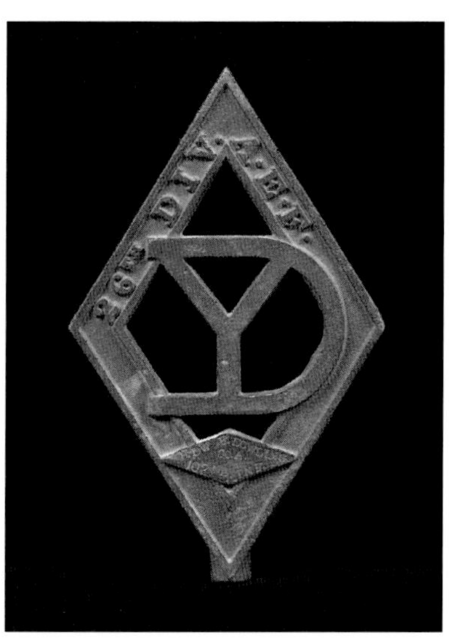

Grave marker, cast metal. A metal sign like this was purchased, engraved (or stamped) and inserted onto a rod at a veteran's grave site. This one was made for Edward F. Dowling of Company A, 102nd Regiment, 26th Yankee Division. Dowling survived the war but likely died in the years closely following the end of wartime, when veterans were still participating in memorial events. *Courtesy of the West Haven Veterans Museum & Learning Center.*

Starita, Kider (Company I, 316th Infantry), d. November 11, 1918
St. Germain, Wilfred C. (Headquarters Battery, 114th Field Artillery), d. November 11, 1918
Stratton, William A. (Company E, 23rd Infantry), d. July 18, 1918
Street, John Philip (Major), killed in action, date unknown
Streit, Christian (U.S. Navy), d. October 4, 1918
Strickland, Paul S. (Lieutenant, Machine Gun Battalion, 39th Infantry), d. July 21, 1918
Sullivan, Michael J. (Private, Company M, 316th Infantry), d. December 18, 1918
Sullivan, Thomas F. (Private, Company C, 102nd Infantry), d. September 26, 1918
Swanson, Albert M. (Private, Company M, 23rd Infantry), d. July 7, 1918
Swanson, Paul A. (Private, Company K, 18th Infantry), d. July 18, 1918
Tate, William (22nd Company, 152nd Depot Brigade), d. October 15, 1918
Taylor, Robert (Private), died of wounds, date unknown
Teitelman, Nathan (Company F, 26th Infantry), d. July 22, 1918
Thompson, Clyde (Company B, 102nd Infantry), d. July 23, 1918
Thompson, Lester H. (Private, Company E, 807th Pioneer Infantry), d. August 15, 1918
Thompson, Thomas A. (Company F, 2nd Battalion, Edgewood Arsenal, MD), d. September 30, 1918
Tinker, William George, Jr. (Private, Company F, 102nd Infantry), d. August 5, 1918
Titus, Clifford C. (Private), killed in action, date unknown
Toole, Henry J. (Coxswain, U.S. Navy), d. June 8, 1919
Tramontano, Alfonso (Company G, 316th Infantry), d. October 24, 1918
Trecher, Edward B. (Private), died of wounds, date unknown
Trumbull, John F. (Major, 60th Engineers), d. October 17, 1918
Tuttle, Philip E. (Charleston Detachment U.S. Marine Corps), d. August 1, 1918
Tylus, Joe (Private), killed in action, date unknown
Upson, Robert M. (Corporal, Headquarters Battery, 6th Field Artillery), d. January 21, 1918
Vaughan, John J. (Private, 2nd Heavy Motor Ordnance Repair Shop Company), d. October 17, 1918
Verderame, Joseph (Private, Company E, 102nd Infantry), d. September 11, 1918
Vicchia, Michael D. (Private), killed in action or died of accident, date unknown

Vinoski, Frank C. (Company B, 102nd Infantry), d. October 17, 1918
Virgilio, Salvatore (Private, Machine Gun Company, 102nd Infantry), d. July 23, 1918
Walker, Raymond A. (Lieutenant, Dental Corps), d. September 16, 1918
Walpole, Thomas J. (Company F, 9th Infantry), d. November 10, 1918
Walpole, William F. (Battery F, 302nd Field Artillery), d. February 21, 1919
Warner, Stephen R. (Lieutenant, Aviation Service), d. April 26, 1918
Watkins, Ira C. (Horseshoer, Company D, 103rd Machine Gun Battalion), d. April 27, 1918
Weiss, Nathan (First Provisional Company, Ordnance Detachment), d. October 23, 1918
Williamson, William P. (152nd Depot Brigade), d. September 29, 1918
Wilson, Ruel Edward (2nd Company, CSI, Aviation Service), d. February 1, 1918
Wise, Walter H. (Corporal, Company M, 159th Infantry), d. January 16, 1918
Zaracovitis, Costas (Corporal, Company M, 102nd Infantry), d. July 22, 1918

Lest We Forget.

New Haven World War I veterans medal. The reverse of the medal reads, "To her sons who went forth to war that their homes might remain at peace, 1917–1919." *Courtesy of the West Haven Veterans Museum & Learning Center.*

BIBLIOGRAPHY

Books, Articles and Programs

American Battle Monuments Commission, Brookwood American Cemetery, n.d.

Bausum, Anne. *Sergeant Stubby: How a Stray Dog and His Best Friend Helped Win World War I and Stole the Heart of a Nation*. Washington, D.C.: National Geographic, 2014.

Brandon, Laura. *Art & War*. New York: Palgrave Macmillan, 2007.

Brown, Elizabeth Mills. *New Haven: A Guide to Architecture and Urban Design*. New Haven, CT: Yale University Press, 1976.

Cornish, Paul. *The First World War Galleries*. London, UK: Imperial War Museum, 2014.

Cruttwell, C.R.M.F. *A History of the Great War, 1914–1918*. 2nd ed. Chicago: Academy Chicago Publishers, 1991.

Dodd, Philip. "War and Modern Memory." *Free Thinking*, BBC 3, July 13, 2016.

Gillis, John R. *Commemorations: The Politics of National Identity*. Princeton, NJ: Princeton University Press, 1994.

Graves, Robert. *Good-Bye to All That*. London, UK: Penguin Classics, 2014.

Hauslee, W.M., F.G. Howe and A.C. Doyle. *Soldiers of the Great War*. Vol. 1. Washington, D.C.: Soldiers Record Publishing Association, 1920.

Hawkins-Dady, Mark, ed. *The WWI Centenary Exhibition*. London, UK: Imperial War Museum, 2015.

Hitchcock, W.H. "A Popular Painter of American Public Men." *Illustrated American*, September 11, 1897.

Jerome, Elizabeth Maude. *Lieut. Gilbert Nelson Jerome*. Np: privately printed, 1920.

Lloyd, David W. *Battlefield Tourism, Pilgrimage and the Commemoration of the Great War in Britain, Australia and Canada, 1919–1939*. Oxford, UK: Berg, 1998.

Lowell, A. Lawrence. *New England Aviators, 1914–1918, Their Portraits and Their Records*. Boston: Houghton Mifflin Company, 1919.

Macaluso, Laura A. "Art for the Elm City: Public Art in New Haven, Connecticut." PhD diss., Salve Regina University, 2016.

McDonald, Amy Athey. "Yale Collections Are Time Capsules of the People, Politics, and Propaganda of WWI." *Yale News*, August 25, 2014.

Morgan, Gaby, ed. *Poems from the First World War*. London, UK: Macmillan Books, 2013.

Mosse, George L. *Fallen Soldiers: Reshaping the Memory of the World Wars*. New York: Oxford University Press, 1990.

Sibley, Frank P. *With the Yankee Division in France*. Boston: Little, Brown, and Company, 1919.

Storey, Neil R. *Animals in the First World War*. Oxford, UK: Shire Publications, 2014.

Strickland, Daniel. *Connecticut Fights: The Story of the 102nd Regiment*. New Haven, CT: Quinnipiack Press, 1930.

Tooley, Hunt. *The Great War, Western Front and Home Front*. 2nd ed. London, UK: Palgrave Macmillan, 2016.

U.S. Army. *American Armies and Battlefields in Europe*. Washington, D.C.: Center for Military History, 1995.

Van Ells, Mark D. *America and WWI, A Traveler's Guide*. Northampton, MA: Interlink Books Inc., 2015.

Williamson, Harold F. *Winchester, the Gun that Won the West*. Washington, D.C.: Combat Forces Press, 1952.

Wingate, Jennifer. *Sculpting Doughboys, Memory, Gender, and Taste in America's World War I Memorials*. Burlington, VT: Ashgate, 2013.

Archival Documents and Collections

English, Philip, War Diary 1917–1919, Whitney Library, New Haven Museum.

European War Folders, New Haven Local History Room, New Haven Free Public Library.

Evergreen Cemetery Records.

Jennie Gilbert Jerome Family Papers, 1858–1979, MSS 130, Whitney Library, New Haven Museum.

Jerome Family Papers, circa 1824–1956, MS 0762, Mount Holyoke College, Archives and Special Collections.

Military Service Records, State of Connecticut.

New Haven Military Collection, MSS 80, Whitney Library, New Haven Museum.

Program, Dedication of World War Memorial and Honor Roll, New Haven Green, May 30, 1929.

Stubby "A.E.F" Scrapbook, National Museum of American History, Smithsonian Institution.

Stubby Folder, New Britain Public Library.

War Records Department, Historical Data Filed, State Archives Record Group No. 012, Connecticut State Library.

World War I Collection, MS 754, Manuscripts & Archives, Yale University Library.

Image, Museum and Private Collections

Audio Preservation Fund

City of New Haven

Connecticut Historical Society

Connecticut State Library and Museum

Dillon, John T., Esq.

Greenberg, Robert S., Made in New Haven

Imperial War Museum, London

Library of Congress

Local History Room, New Haven Public Library

Macaluso, Laura A.

Manuscript & Archives, Yale University Library

Metropolitan Museum of Art

Mount Holyoke College Archives and Special Collections

National Museum of American History, Smithsonian Institution

National WWI Museum and Memorial

New England Air Museum

West Haven Veterans Museum & Learning Center
Whitney Library & New Haven Museum
Yale University Art Gallery

INDEX

ABOUT THE AUTHOR

Laura A. Macaluso, PhD, holds degrees in art history and the humanities from Southern Connecticut State University, Syracuse University in Italy and Salve Regina University. She has worked as a grants writer and curator in historic sites, museums and art and park organizations. She held a Fulbright at the Swaziland National Museum in 2008–9 and returned in 2010 under an Ambassador's Fund for Cultural Preservation award from the State Department. She curated the exhibit "An Artist at War: Deane Keller, New Haven's Monuments Man" and authored the accompanying article in *Connecticut Explored* magazine (Winter 2014–15). Laura is the author of *Historic Treasures of New Haven: Celebrating 375 Years of the Elm City* (The History Press, 2013) and *Art of the Amistad and the Portrait of Cinqué*, published by the American Association of State and Local History/ Rowman & Littlefield (March 2016). In addition, she has written articles, blog posts and book reviews for *Material Culture, The International Society for Landscape, Place, and Material Culture*; *Nineteenth Century*; AASLH; National Council on Public History; *Collections, A Journal for Museum and Archives Professionals*; and Adventures in Preservation. She lives with her husband, Jeffrey Nichols, the president and chief executive officer of Thomas Jefferson's Poplar Forest, in Lynchburg, Virginia.